I'll Get That Job!

I'll Get That Job!

A REAL GUIDE FROM REAL EXPERTS ON GETTING THE JOB YOU WANT!

Paolo Casamassima

ISBN: 1508842027
ISBN 13: 9781508842026
Library of Congress Control Number: 2015904928
CreateSpace Independent Publishing Platform
North Charleston, South Carolina

Selected quotes

"**L**ooking for a job is a full-time job." Dr. Vishwajeet Rana, Greensea Capital Investment Bank

"See every interview opportunity as practice for the next role, and eventually you will find your role." Tosin Ojikutu, Investec

"When writing a CV, too many candidates focus on themselves; however, the organization needs to know how the organization will benefit by hiring this person. Put yourself in the manager's shoes." Pritul Khagram, People Force International

"Networking is extremely important. The job an individual can land is more and more the result of his or her network. The first five to eight years of experience are spent in improving one's own technical skill set; however, the successive twenty years of career are heavily influenced by networking skills. Having a network only in your company or your sector is very dangerous." Cristiano Cardarelli, Contract Excellence Manager

"If you apply to an organization, check if you know anyone who works there. Finding a job is easier if you can prove to a prospective employer that you can do the job and if there is someone credible who knows the hiring manager and can vouch for how good you are—that does more than a CV ever could. Also, the more visible you are online the better your access to opportunity and your knowledge of the market." Victoria Barry-Woods, Allegis Group

"When applying for a job, knowing your audience is very important!" Sheryl Cusia, Boudicca Proxy

"How to get a job? In a nutshell, you need to stand out! Your CV has to be good—have a good CV, spend more time writing your CV, and get your CV looking good." Anonymous financial industry recruiter, London

Acknowledgments

I dedicate this book to my beautiful wife, Yulia, for her ongoing
support and encouragement and for making
me believe in myself.
To my loving parents, who were my first
supporters and my biggest fans
and who helped me to become what I am today.
To uncle Antonio, who passed on to me his passion for writing.
I also want to thank all of the respondents to my
survey who took the
time to speak with me and answer my questions.
Finally, I want to thank Cristiano Cardarelli,
who not only provided me
an amazing insight into my research topic but also helped me
with the final review of the book.

Table of Contents

Introduction

Who is this book for?

As a manager in charge of the recruitment of a large team located in various countries and continents, I have noticed how, after the 2008 financial crisis, the volume of CVs I receive for each position I recruit for has dramatically increased, quadrupled at least. I have been impressed with the number of overqualified graduates who invest vast sums of money in their education and have two master's degrees by the age of twenty-five. Despite this, their curriculum vitaes (also known as CVs or résumés) are often appalling and their career goals are far from clear. I am also puzzled and concerned about the number of middle-aged people coming from a round of layoffs who, despite having stellar CVs, apply for relatively junior or even entry-level positions. Some have worked for more than twenty years; they have probably not touched their CVs in ten years and have no clue about what to do. As one of my interviewees said at the early stages of my research for this book, "Some people write improper CVs despite having worked in an industry for twenty or thirty years. This does not help their chances when they send out their CVs. Recruiters and hiring managers will have to sift through the CV trying to understand them. And we just do not want to do that." How does one get a job, then? Even get an interview? Be noticed by a company? I wrote this book to help three categories of job seekers:

- **The young graduate**, who needs to know how to get started in order to find a job and improve his or her CV;
- **The middle-aged person**, who has been laid off recently, perhaps unexpectedly, and needs to find a job in an environment that has changed dramatically during the last ten or fifteen years; and
- **The career changer**, who has decided for various reasons to change careers (whether within the same industry or not) but struggles to get the attention of potential employers.

I have interviewed a number of team managers, human resource (HR) professionals, and headhunters in various industries, sectors, and countries, looking for answers that job hunters can use to increase their chances of getting jobs. Through this book I wish to show the job seeker what really goes through the mind of the hiring manager and recruiter while he or she looks through piles of CVs for potential candidates.

There are plenty of books and articles about job searching. I believe, however, that many of them were written before 2008 (when Lehman Brothers collapsed and the subsequent financial crisis began in many countries) and before the advent of new online technologies such as LinkedIn that have revolutionized the way people look for jobs. So, to provide context and background to this book, I will begin, in chapter 1, by looking at the way the job market currently operates, highlighting its new characteristics, problems, and opportunities for job seekers.

Chapters 2 and 3 will cover some of the most important elements of the job search process, the writing of a CV and cover letters and the recruiting process itself with all of its participants. In chapter 4 I will move on to discuss one of the most powerful ways of securing a job, networking. Chapter 5 details the job interview, highlighting common mistakes to avoid and techniques to use to impress the interviewer.

In chapters 6 and 7, we look into two major categories of job seekers. Chapter 6 focuses on the recent graduate who has relatively little to no work experience. Chapter 7 focuses on the career changer, a person who moves from one industry to another, continuing to apply the same skills, or stays in the same industry but tries to change roles, or even changes both roles and industries.

Chapter 8, "Final recommendations from the experts", is a list of the best advice on job searching from some of the people interviewed for this book.

Aim and structure of the book

This book aims to analyze the changing dynamics of the job market and help the reader in getting a job.

I have chosen to write a short book because, if you have decided to invest your money in a book about job searching, you are probably already tired of sending out CVs without success and you want answers, quickly, about how to get a job. There are many myths about what employers look for in a candidate. Job seekers need to think about how best to tailor their searches, based on how decision makers really think rather than how the media tells us they think. Most importantly, this book aims to explain to job seekers that there are no winning formulas or standard rules for landing a job. Instead, there are trends. There is no special CV, no cover letter, no winning sentence that will help you get a job. You may be the most amazing candidate for the job, but ultimately you need to fit into the framework that the company has created to identify the ideal candidate. You might not fit one single criterion and therefore be out of the running for a specific job. Getting a job takes hard work, dedication, and commitment. Getting a job requires believing in yourself even though you know somebody else out there knows how to do the job better than you do. Getting a job means showing your next employer that you will be humble and that you will be able to adapt, no matter where you are moving from and no matter what your experience is. Getting a job means sending hundreds of CVs, trying them in various formats, testing cover letters, speaking to people, being visible, and not giving up after hundreds of unsuccessful applications. You must have the resilience of a telemarketer!

Recruiters and hiring managers just do not have the time to even reply to all candidates that apply for a job. I get an average of two hundred e-mails per day; do you think I reply to all of them? Very often we advertise a position asking for a specific skill, but nonetheless we will receive lots of CVs without that skill. The problem is that the customer for headhunters is not the job seeker; their customer is the company looking for candidates, who ultimately become the product. The recruiter will only look at the best products, which will be bought by his or her customers. People are desperate and therefore will keep on sending CVs thinking "someone will see my CV and call me." Nowadays you need to be relentless; you cannot give up! Even if you see a door close, you have to keep going. Send your CV directly to banks and HRs, and go onto LinkedIn to find out who is the direct recruiter for xyz institution.

Anonymous financial industry recruiter,
London, United Kingdom

This book aims to open people's eyes to the changing dynamics of the job market. Artificial intelligence is changing the way people operate in their day-to-day activities. Repetitive tasks are increasingly being automated and, only when unavoidable, outsourced to countries with lower labor costs. Despite all these factors, getting a job is still a people's power. There will always be need for at least some employees who have the right mix of skills. However, the job market can currently absorb only a certain number of people. How do you ensure you are one of those people? Either you come from a top university and have access to the best opportunities, or you need to find another way to shine. Ultimately, whoever shines more gets the job. How can you shine? Good grades from a good university are important but no longer enough. You need languages and a completely new mentality. Humility and adaptability are viewed positively by all employers. Flexibility, in terms of both how you can adjust within a company and how ready you are to move, is important. You need to be visible, building a strong network and having an online presence on LinkedIn. Mobility can also be extremely important. Great jobs do not always appear within close range, within the same city, close to family or friends. Jobs may exist in a different city or country from the one where you live, and you might have to adjust to frequent travel or moving your family if you want the job.

The main issue for companies today is that they struggle to find the skills and the talent they need. Having knowledge of IT applications can be useful, because a company can utilize your extra IT skills for a small task instead of hiring another person or outsourcing the job. The key is to become a person who anticipates the company's future need and solves the problem, or, said differently, anticipates a problem and makes sure it will be solved before it even arises. Plenty of jobs do not yet exist but are created by the situation. You should be recruited not necessarily for the skills you currently have but for the skills you will acquire in the company. In a world that is more and more uncertain, you need to be able to cope with uncertainty to have a good future.

In my latest few years as manager, I have interviewed a large number of people and probably seen several hundred CVs. But do I manage hundreds of people? No, I do not. I started writing this book while managing a relatively large team of equity researchers, fifteen to eighteen people, with the number fluctuating due to interns and temporary staff. I then managed even larger teams, but later moved back to managing a smaller team. The dynamic I experience is similar whether within a larger or a smaller team: each time I post a job opening, I am bombarded by CVs from people who have many different levels of skill and motivation. Applicants include recent bachelor's degree graduates and PhD candidates, people with twenty or more years of experience who are looking for a career change, and people who have never worked, people with experience in varying sectors, and people who have worked for a competitor firm within my industry. They have several levels of motivation but two things in common. The first is that they need a job for reasons ranging from the need to support their families to the desire for a prestigious career. They may have more or less experience than I do, and they may speak more or fewer languages than I do. But again, the one thing they have in common is that they all need a job. What is the second thing they have in common? They write their CVs from their point of view, not mine. A candidate could possess skills that are important to me; however, unaware of what I am looking for, he or she may deem them unimportant and thus not include them in the CV. Candidates often do not try to think about what I, my team, or my organization need. Pritul Khagram (People Force International) states, "When writing a CV, too many candidates focus on themselves; the organization, however, needs to know how it will benefit from hiring this person." Many candidates attend the job interview thinking they have done and seen it all during their work experience, so they can do any job. At the same time, many new graduates believe they are capable of the same thing just because they have recently finished the relevant courses. But what really happens in my mind and in the minds of millions of managers, HR professionals, and headhunters when they look for a candidate?

This book does not aim to give you the final answer. There is no final answer, because each sector is different, every hiring manager is different, and the same manager could act in different ways depending on the sector for which he is recruiting. However, trends exist. This book is intended to show you the trends across various industries that, if properly understood and managed, will help you get a job. This book will highlight certain strategies, things to do or say, methods, and tips that will most likely increase your possibilities of getting a job. There are, of course, also things that you should never do, things that once done will certainly compromise your chances of getting a job with that specific organization. We will highlight those as well.

Networking

I have explained that there are no fixed guidelines and no magic word, CV, or cover letter template that will guarantee you a job or even an interview. However, in nearly all of the interviews I have conducted for this book, the one element that stands out in terms of giving the candidate a better chance of getting a job is the number of connections the person has. Connections are extremely important. A professional is only as good as his or her network. In many sectors today, if you do not have a network you do not exist. Having connections only within your company or your sector can be very dangerous.

Networking is critical in finding a job. However, networking doesn't come out of nowhere. You must work on building your network. Surprisingly, most people I know have never networked. When I studied at university several years ago, nobody ever mentioned how important networking would be to finding a job.

What is networking? It defines you as a professional. It is your present and future career. It is the number of business opportunities that you can bring to a business or create for yourself. It is the number of people whose problems you have solved or with whom you have worked to solve other people's problems. Your network will help you to make a sale, to get in touch with a senior manager, and eventually to get you a job. It is the number of people with whom you share a common interest or even just a common contact. According to most of the recruitment specialists interviewed for this book, it is thanks to networking that people secure jobs, regardless of the sector, field, or position. "It is all about who you know. Build a connection with a person in the industry you want to work in, get into the circle of contacts, and get yourself known. Think to yourself as one would in a movie: if people like it, they will tell others about it," states Pritul Khagram of People Force International. The power of networking and the various methods for networking will be described further in chapter 4.

CHAPTER 1

Looking for a job in the current economic environment

A s the first anniversary of her graduation with a degree in ecotourism and cultural history approached, Seren Johnson[1] was still jobless and frustrated. When she finished her studies at one of Sweden's top universities, she had accepted an unpaid, part-time position at a nonprofit organization focused on human rights and tourism, hoping it would lead to a full-time job with a salary. When her contract ended, she declined the offer to stay on as an unpaid intern. Since then, dozens of applications and endless hours of networking have yielded just two interviews, despite a CV boasting a stellar academic record and a string of hard-to-obtain internships.

Lindsey Callaghan[1] graduated from LUISS University in Rome and then took two years to find a job even slightly related to her experience. Her contract with ENI, the largest oil company in Italy, is currently renewing monthly. "Many of my former university colleagues are in the same or a worse situation; the only thing I would recommend to graduates is to be patient and keep trying," she says.

Youth unemployment rates in some EU countries are scandalously high; the situations faced by Seren Johnson and Lindsey Callaghan are a reflection of the depth of the Western world's economic crisis. At

---

1 Fictitious name to protect the identity of the interviewee.

present, Europe probably has the most well-educated generation in its history. Parents have invested a lot of money in the their children's education and done everything right, but when the children complete their studies, society tells them they have no future. The problem not only of unemployment but also underemployment—including workers who are overqualified for their current jobs, interns who are unpaid or underpaid, and part-time employees who want full-time work—has reached critical levels in many EU countries and could leave a permanent financial and psychological mark on an entire generation.

In an article published on June 26, 2013, Gavin Hewitt of BBC News commented, "Whilst Europe debates how jobs are created, tens of thousands of young Europeans are on the move in search of work. They are part of a great migration. It is, however, often the best and brightest who are emigrating. In the year up to April 2012, 87,000 people left Ireland. Many moved to Australia and New Zealand. Most of them had achieved high levels of education. Some may return. Many will not. The fear is of a brain drain, which will leave some of these European countries stagnating.[2]"

Underemployment drives people into poverty and ultimately onto welfare. The process of becoming self-sufficient through employment is taking longer than it previously did. Recent graduates often receive low income, therefore low living standards, and end up in poverty, relying on other types of income—such as welfare and health benefits—to support themselves. While unemployment is a known cause of psychological and social problems, the mental effects of underemployment are less well researched. But experts say they are equally serious. Daniel Feldman, who has written several books examining underemployment, lists cynicism, resentment, anxiety, and depression as some of the common, long-lasting side effects.[3]

---

2 Gavin Hewitt, "Jobs Crisis: Europe's Great Migration," *BBC News*, June 26, 2013, http://www.bbc.co.uk/news/world-europe-23047678.

3 Douglas C. Maynard and Daniel C. Feldman, *Underemployment: Psychological, Economic, and Social Challenges* (New York: Springer, 2011).

The 2008 crisis

In 2008 an important financial event took place. Lehman Brothers, one of the largest banking giants, collapsed. The difference between the associated financial crisis and those of the past is that the 2008 crisis reached a global scale, affecting banks and economies worldwide. Lehman Brothers had always been considered so large that it could not fail. The 2008 crisis was, therefore, a shocking to the core of the banking industry. It has affected so many people, institutions, and industries because so much equity and debt was secured by the banks that subsequently failed or at least experienced hardship.

> *This is a different financial crisis because it is longer. It is so strong that it has changed the world. I was hired in 2008 by my previous employer, and I knew I would be responsible for growth and expansion. As soon as the crisis started, I was told I had to start talking to employees about layoffs. Within twelve hours, from "buy-buy-expansion" we moved to "sell-sell-layoffs." This crisis has been like a meteorite, a heartquake.*
> Stefano Bottaro, Opera Theatre of Rome

Since the 2008 crisis, the world has changed. The Western economies have changed. When talking about economic downturns, it is important to contextualize them. We continue to see growth in Asia and emerging markets. On the other hand, we see a partial economic downturn in the United States and a lot of economic downturn in Europe. While the United States is currently still experiencing a postcrisis bubble, a dramatic effect following speculation in commodities, Europe has clear fiscal problems. The two continents are also not consuming their own output in full. Although in the past the United States and Europe exported a large proportion of their production to other countries, emerging markets have now entered the exporting game but are also producing more and exporting less.

The phenomenon of outsourcing

Another major trend is the phenomenon of outsourcing. Famous consulting firms and business courses have made outsourcing a must, a great business strategy to increase output and reduce costs. We have moved all lower-value services and jobs away from the Western world. We do not simply speak about outsourcing. In most cases, the outsourcing is an offshoring to third-world countries where labor cost is a fraction of labor cost in the country where the company is based. Although firms in the IT-, legal-, and financial-services industries outsource only entry-level positions, some firms engaged in the production of consumer goods outsource the majority of their production. "We outsource most of the production to third-world countries, roughly 80 percent. If we need more employees for a certain type of clothing, we will outsource where the cost of labor is cheaper. If the manufacturing of a particular item is done by machinery, we move its production where the cost of energy is lower" (Antonio Iandolo, DB Apparel). Adding value starts in a recurring manner from a small core. Value is added from already existing value. In the job market, for example, you need people who start at a low level who will progressively add value and move up. In the Western world, we have removed all low-value jobs in an effort to reduce costs.

> We moved away plants, call centers, admin, etc. What happens then? You need workers, lower salaries who spend in the local area. These people are no longer there and hence, they do not spend in taxes either. You do not see many rich high fliers or VPs spending money in their local markets. Slowly we have created a bigger gap between the rich and the poor. The reason we have so many CVs from young people is that the jobs that we have outsourced would have absorbed them. Nobody ever thinks about the "off-balance-sheet" factor. A company can save $3.00 per hour by outsourcing, but how much does it cost the government that a job that has been moved away? You do not have any more revenues coming in from this person, but you need to

stimulate these people to work. The cost is even higher to the government in terms of both incentives and taxes not being paid. The young population has no access to the job market, because the job market has been moved away. The older population, in most cases, speaks only one language, meaning they can do business only in their country.

Cristiano Cardarelli, Contract Excellence Manager

Many changes happened in the last three to five years. It is all about bargaining power now. There is a lot of cost cutting, many jobs are being moved to cost-cutting centers, and not many positions are available compared to the past. There is more supply than demand. Much of this is caused by outsourcing. For example, in my previous organization the entire Finance and HR departments were moved to Budapest, and all people within those departments were made redundant.

Pritul Khagram, People Force International

A more entrepreneurial society

The times when people used to get a job and stay in it until retirement are long gone. The full-time, permanent employment bubble has burst. People now have to adjust. The sooner they realize the job market has changed the better. Many professionals have told me that society is gradually becoming more entrepreneurial.

This is a time for people to be creative. There are so many resources at low cost nowadays; you can be creative and start a business. People, whatever job they have, should work as hard as possible and learn as much as possible. People should use all their opportunities to challenge themselves to learn something new. I always tell my staff to excel no matter where they are. It is elementary, but in all jobs there is an element of fun. You find it, and that's it! I used to work at Starbucks, and I enjoyed becoming an awesome barista. I learned how to make great coffees and then challenged myself to make thirty cappuccinos in one minute. Every time you have a free moment, try to learn something new.

Sheryl Cusia, Boudicca Proxy

While the term entrepreneurial usually refers to people who have the courage to leave their comfort zone and set up a business, today this also refers to being an entrepreneurial job seeker. According to Julia Barber of Cornell Partnership, "things have changed, because people have much more flexible working conditions, are able to adjust to part-time or flexible work, temporary contracts, consulting jobs, and so forth. The bottom line is that the crisis has made everyone much more entrepreneurial; people do more jobs in less time. It all comes down to how much you want to be visible in the market and how much you are willing to adjust." The workplace landscape has changed markedly as a result of the downturn. In most cases, people will not be able to find their dream jobs; they will not send a handful of applications and land a job immediately after university. Finding a job will be a long process of hard work. "Looking for a job is a full-time job," states Dr. Vishwajeet Rana of Greensea Capital Investment Bank.

To a degree, finding a job is a numbers game. The more applications you send the more chances you will have to get a job. When you apply for a job, you are putting yourself up against God knows how many people. The candidate should not be worried about going to an interview for a job he will not get. It is important to interview for the experience. It is very noticeable when a person has not had an interview in a while.

Julia Barber, Cornell Partnership

Career progression is not guaranteed, because many organizations are flat. Employees will not be guaranteed a nice management position in a few years down the line. People need to work harder, be prepared to travel, be creative, and be ready to do the unexpected.

The current financial crisis is not a crisis; it is structural change. There are many positions that no longer exist or are disappearing. What can you do then? Move, change, travel, get middle positions, and think that you might have to stay there and not progress. It is no longer guaranteed to have a career and a management position within ten years of starting at the same company.

Marco Sartarelli, MS Partners

Summary

1. Youth unemployment rates in some EU countries are scandalously high despite an extremely well-educated generation. The problem is not only unemployment but also underemployment—including workers who are overqualified for their current jobs, interns who are unpaid or underpaid, and part-time employees who want full-time work.
2. Tens of thousands of young Europeans are on the move in search of work. It is often the best and brightest who are emigrating, and many will not return to their home countries. There is fear of a brain drain that will leave some European countries stagnating.
3. Underemployment drives people into poverty and ultimately onto welfare. The process of becoming self-sufficient through employment is taking longer than it previously did. Recent graduates often receive low income, therefore low living standards, and end up in poverty, relying on other types of income such as welfare and health benefits to support themselves.
4. The job market has changed dramatically since the fall of Lehman Brothers in 2008. The current financial crisis is not

a crisis; it is structural change. There are many positions that no longer exist or are disappearing. People have much more flexible working conditions and need to adjust to part-time, flexible work, temporary contracts, consulting jobs, and so forth. The crisis has made everyone much more entrepreneurial.

5. Career progression is no longer guaranteed, because many organizations are flat and do not necessarily promote from within. The times when people used to get a job and stay in it until retirement are long gone. The full-time, permanent employment bubble has burst.

6. The phenomenon of outsourcing is one of the key issues challenging Western economies and job markets. Many companies offshore to third-world countries most of the lower-value services and jobs. These jobs used to be given to young graduates, who now struggle to find entry positions simply because they have been outsourced.

7. Finding a job has become a numbers game. The more applications you send, the higher the chances of getting a job.

8. It is important to be an entrepreneurial job seeker. Things have changed because people have much more flexible working conditions, are able to adjust to part-time or flexible work, temporary contracts, consulting jobs, and so forth. The bottom line is that the crisis has made everyone much more entrepreneurial; people do more jobs in less time. It all comes down to how much you want to be visible in the market and how much you are willing to adjust.

CHAPTER 2

Curriculum Vitae vs. Cover Letters

If you do not have the ability to create a good CV, get somebody to do it for you. Make the investment.
Cristiano Cardarelli, Contract Excellence Manager

The curriculum vitae (also known as the CV or résumé), is one of the most important documents you will ever produce in your life. To be blunt, most people need money in life and need a job to earn it. The CV is the key to getting that job. The better the CV, the better the chance of getting the work you want. The CV may include a cover letter along with other details that are important when applying for international jobs, fellowships, grants, and research, scientific, and academic positions. Both the CV and the cover letter offer the potential employer a snapshot of who you are and why you may be qualified for the position.

The CV highlights a person's qualifications for employment in a particular job or career field. It is an individually designed summary, usually one or two pages, of the person's personal, educational, and work experience qualifications as they relate to the employment sought. It should be an honest, concise, well-organized presentation of the candidate, his or her interests, skills, abilities, and accomplishments. The candidate must be able to demonstrate (if needed) that the CV is a true reflection of his or her knowledge and skills. Honesty is critical.

The cover letter is a business letter. It gives you an opportunity to introduce yourself to the prospective employer, express your interest in the position, and present your value proposition for a job. It offers the employer an insight into your personality through your writing style, and gives you an opportunity to impress the employer with your communication skills. The cover letter is an introduction to yourself with regard to the job opening. Cover letters are generally a half page to one page in length, divided into a header, introduction, body, and closing. The cover letter should contain enough details to complement the CV and interest the person reading it. "Cover letters should include why the candidate is interested in the job and why the person would add value to the organization. I read the cover letter first; the CV is about ten times more important than the cover letter," states Michael O'Brien of BNY Mellon.

When cover letters are "too perfect," it makes me suspicious. I want to get to know the candidate for real, and the "ready-to-use" expressions and answers normally mean I am facing a wall. We all have strengths and weaknesses that make us a good fit for some jobs. If we are not real about them, we might get the job. It's a pity that it might be not the right job. And that's a pity for both employer and employee.

Mishelle Sassun, Bee Creations

Based on my recruitment experience as well as most of the answers received from our expert panel, cover letters are becoming less and less important. This is because recruiters and recruiting managers have to go through a very large volume of CVs each time they work on a job opening. Managers will hardly look at a cover letter, and headhunters will not look at it.

With regard to cover letters, I honestly do not read them at all. There is only one person whose cover letter I remember; most cover letters all look the same.

Sheryl Cusia, Boudicca Proxy

I do not read cover letters. The personal statement in the CV is very important. What did you do? What are your skills? What are your long term objectives? These are the key points a personal statement must answer.

Antonio Iandolo, DB Apparel

Every CV should be a reflection of the individual, so for me there is no set template or formula that I would like to see as a hiring manager. I tend to skim through the letters and jump straight to the experience.

Tosin Ojikutu, Investec

As a recruiter I would say we hardly read cover letters, and we do not forward them to our clients. We do not look at cover letters, because we (recruiters) are the cover letters. We look at very specific skills, and the client pays us for this. Cover letters can be helpful, but keep it short; it is a dangerous zone. Do not mention "getting involved in the values of the company" and all that kind of stuff. Be short and structured. Mention three things: a) why you are applying, b) your qualities, and c) your goals.

Julia Barber, Cornell Partnership

We do not read cover letters at all. You should just apply and include the following sentence: "Please find attached my CV. I currently work at xyz covering the following areas: xxx." Most important is the CV. You need to stand out! Your CV has to be good—have a good CV, spend more time writing your CV, and get your CV looking good.

Anonymous financial recruiter, London, United Kingdom

Why writing cover letters?

I believe people should approach the writing of cover letters based on the type of job search they are pursuing. Across my network I have come across two types of job seekers. The first one will apply to hundreds of job postings at the same time, effectively playing a numbers game. This strategy can work very well in some cases, especially when the candidate has outstanding accomplishments or, if junior, has studied at top universities. Candidates who are much more thorough about their job search will usually passively observe the market until they see something that really interests them. When this "perfect match" or "dream job" becomes available, they will take the time to tailor the CV and write an outstanding cover letter. Although cover letters appear to have become less important, and most recruiters and hiring managers will not have the chance to even look at them, my view is that if you are applying for only a handful of jobs you should not miss the opportunity to write a cover letter, and perhaps you should make an effort to write a really outstanding one. Some job applicants believe that their experience should speak for itself, that the qualifications on their CV should say it all. In some rare cases, that could be true. Regardless, the rigid structure of a CV will not give your personality the opportunity to shine. The cover letter is, therefore, your chance to introduce yourself as a person rather than just a set of skills. If that cover letter will not be read, no worries. But what do you have to lose?

How to write a CV

CV—LENGTH

Most of our panel of experts believe that the CV must be between one and two pages depending on the level of the position. An alternative is to have both a one-page version and a two-page version. The CV should never be three pages. "Obviously, when it is an entry level position one page is more than enough," states Julia Faida of Optimum Media. "A one-page CV for people with less than five years of experience; two pages once experience has increased," states Michael Witte of Capgemini. Some managers, however, are those type of super-busy individuals who do recruitment in addition to several other responsibilities and go through a quicker screening process; hence, they prefer shorter CVs. "We prefer a single-page CV; as it catches our interest, we will always request a face-to-face meeting with the potential applicant and request more information then," states Faiz Nazerali of Intellitech I.T. Solutions Ltd. Three-page CVs are usually disregarded because they show that the candidate is unable to determine the relevant skills to highlight his or her fit with the requirements of the new job. Additionally, such a long CV could show the candidate's inability to summarize, which implies that he or she will not be able to communicate efficiently.

> Based on my experience, I would say that the length should be two pages. I think you would struggle doing a one-page CV. I have seen some really good CVs on one page, but they are rare. I would also recommend that candidates not get funny with formatting and color and ensure that the CV has a clear chronological progression. Finally, the personal statement should not be too long, four to five lines at max.
>
> Julia Barber, Cornell Partnership

For a CV to be at most two pages, especially if you are a more mature candidate, it is important to save space by removing previous jobs or skills that are not related to the job for which you are applying. Previous roles are not very important if they do not reflect who you are now. If the current role is a continuation of your previous role, the previous role is important. If a previous role is not relevant to the position for which you are applying, make the mention extremely brief. In my CV, for example, each job that is not relevant to the role or field for which I am applying is listed in just two lines, one line for the job title and one line for a brief description of the responsibilities. The most important reason for mentioning these irrelevant jobs is to avoid leaving time gaps in the CV. It is important for the CV to be structured and relevant at all times. "A CV is just like a book," states an anonymous financial recruiter in London. "A recruiter looks at the title and maybe, but not always, at the profile. The most important part is what the candidate is doing currently and how it is relevant to the job for which he or she is applying. I don't care what they did ten or fifteen years ago; what I want to know is what they are doing now. If you are currently unemployed, present yourself in your personal statement as a 'motivated individual currently seeking opportunities in the job market due to redundancy.' If you are working in a grocery store while looking for work in finance, do not mention the store. Do not make your CV irrelevant; make it relevant! I will look at it to see what your last role was before redundancy and decide if it was relevant to the job you are currently applying for."

CV—STRUCTURE AND FORMAT

The first half of the CV is the most important part. You need to capture the recruiter's attention immediately. Use facts and begin each of your statements with an action word such as created, implemented, improved, or increased. Within ten seconds of reading a CV, I know if I will interview the candidate. The formatting of a CV is also very important.

Delphine Lecluze, Orient Capital

"The way a CV looks is very important," explains Sheryl Cusia, founder of Boudicca Proxy, because "the way phrases are structured will show how the person will be able to communicate. Never make spelling mistakes!" Cristiano Cardarelli, Contract Excellence Manager, says that "the reader of a CV has twenty seconds to understand if the CV is worth reading after line ten." He continues, "The CV has to be easy to read with a nice margin, nice borders, no pictures, details at the top, and a short presentation of no more than five or six lines providing an overview of the candidate. Why should the person be interested in you? What are your main skills? The first part has to set the tone for the whole CV. It must never be disconnected from the rest of the CV. 'I have these skills, and I have done this and that achieving xyz.' Profile, work experience, and major achievements at the top are the structure many managers prefer to see." Personally, I believe a CV has to strike the right balance between skills or responsibilities and accomplishments. The latter will help the interviewer quantify your ability in a more tangible way. Be careful, though! Do not overstate your accomplishments. The interviewer might be able to investigate whether these accomplishments are real. Be honest, but do not be overly humble. Always try to use strong, robust language to describe your experience.

In his interview, Michael O'Brien of BNY Mellon summarized the key elements and recommended structure of a CV:

1. Contact information,
2. Personal statement,
3. Employment history and accomplishments,
4. Education,
5. Professional qualifications,
6. Certifications, accreditations, and professional memberships,
7. Awards and publications,
8. Computer and technical skills, and
9. Interests (only if there is room in the CV; note that they are less important for older applicants).

CV—PERSONAL STATEMENT

The personal statement is composed of a few sentences at the top of the CV. It is sometimes referred to as a career summary or a personal mission statement.

The personal statement cannot be too long or too short. It needs to make the manager willing to read the rest.
Pritul Khagram, People Force International

The personal statement should include key qualities of the candidate, why the applicant is different; it should show some level of experience and where the person aims to go next.
Sheryl Cusia, Boudicca Proxy

The personal statement should be placed at the start of the CV and should be no longer than five lines. It must be short and positive, highlighting key strengths, skills, and experience. The time to elaborate and give evidence of these is later in the CV.

Amina Malik, Human Resource Manager, London

The personal statement is intended to explain where your career has taken you up to this point and what your ambition is for your next job. In many cases it is just a very brief version of a cover letter, which as has previously mentioned is no longer relevant for many companies. "Speaking in simple terms, the personal statement needs to include who the person is and what the person would like to do or achieve in the future. Also, it needs to include a brief summary of the person's skills and expertise. In our company we do not require cover letters; we focus solely on the CV," states Julia Faida of Optimum Media. The purpose of the personal statement is to show why you would be ideal for the job, so it is important that you tailor your personal statement to the job for which you are applying. Begin with a sentence describing your personality.

The specific statement at the top of the CV documenting the personality one claims to have must flow into the rest of the CV. The remainder of the CV should support that statement. If there are any discrepancies, I have no desire to read the CV any further.

Michael Witte, CAPGEMINI

The personal statement also must include something about the candidate's work experience and career goals. The entire statement must be brief, between four and six lines, and have a consistent voice (decide whether to write about yourself in the first or third person, and stick to it). Citing some of the most important skills one has picked up in his or her career up to this point and giving examples of where they were learned is important. The applicant should make sure that the skills mentioned in the CV are the ones the employer wants. In saying this, we want to emphasize how experience that is not relevant should be either left out of the CV entirely or described in no more than two lines. I once read somewhere that we only need to impress employers slightly to get them to interview us. Approaching it from this perspective is one more way to help reduce the size of a CV.

CV—ORIGINAL AND ATTRACTIVE IDEAS

A recruiter or hiring manager will usually go through a large volume of applications and CVs when filling an opening; very often he or she will decide within ten or twenty seconds whether to call a candidate. You need to ensure that your CV will catch the attention of the hiring manager or the person who makes the final decision. Our experts have given a few interesting tips:

> *Candidates should distinguish themselves by putting bullet points at the top of the CV to highlight main skills, what the person has done, and how the experience is relevant for the job. My preferred structure is having at the top of the CV three main skills that match the specific job; this will tell the hiring manager immediately how you fit. Also, try to describe your experience as "situation-task-action-result."[4] When highlighting a skill, you need to prove what you did and what was achieved as a result. Having a recommendation with your CV (verbal or written) is very valuable if the person can provide evidence that you are a proven resource. That person needs to work for the hiring company, know the hiring manager, or have worked with you in the past; a friend who thinks you are a good person isn't relevant.*
>
> *Victoria Barry-Woods, Allegis Group*

An interesting idea comes from Cristiano Cardarelli, Contract Excellence Manager, who suggests making the cover letter your personal statement: "The cover letter is a letter. In my opinion, it should be the five lines at the top of the CV (the personal statement).

---

4 Situation, task, action, and result is also referred to as the STAR technique. Please refer to the section titled "Competency-based interviews" in chapter 6.

The recruiter or the person doing recruiting for the company would receive usually two hundred or more CVs, so he just could not read them all. Unless you are Gandhi or Mother Teresa, you cannot put anything too interesting in a letter." Amina Malik (Human Resource Manager, London) states, "I find a cover letter is an extension of the CV but in paragraph format and that there is an emphasis on personal skills and why you are interested in working for this company. With a well-written CV, this would already be included in the personal statement or within the job responsibilities."

CV—AN OBVIOUS BUT TRICKY CHECKLIST

When your CV is complete, you will have spent so much time and energy on it that it will look amazing. But there will still be mistakes— perhaps something small or something that could be phrased differently. Good advice is to always have the CV double-checked by someone you trust, if possible, someone within your desired industry. This person will know the appropriate key words and language to use in the CV and will easily spot mistakes or sentences that could be phrased differently to best describe your skills.

We have compiled a quick checklist of questions each job seeker should review before submitting a job application. Most of these points seem self-explanatory, but many candidates fail in at least one of them:

- How good does your CV look?
- How well is the CV formatted?
- Have you included a personal statement in the CV?
- Are you sure there are no spelling mistakes in the CV?
- Is your work experience listed chronologically in the CV, with the most recent at the top?
- Is your message clear in the CV?
- Do you know who will be reading your CV? Will your message be clear to him or her?
- Is your CV at most two pages? Have you removed all irrelevant information?

What puts off managers when reading cover letters and CVs

First and most important, *mistakes in a CV put off hiring managers.* "Depending on the competition for the job, a mistake can lead to automatic disqualification," says Michael O'Brien of BNY Mellon. According to Julia Barber of Cornell Partnership, "managers are put off by bad formatting, excessive punctuation, and fancy colors." "Typos and the lack of succinct phrases put me off," states Tosin Ojikutu of Investec. The CV and cover letter must be relevant to the position for which you are applying and must be filled with interesting facts, skills, and achievements. Tailor the CV to the target company. Limit the skills highlighted in your CV to those relevant to the target job. Many CVs for technical positions erroneously list every system, software program, and technology with which the applicant has ever worked; hence, they distract the recruiting manager from the core competencies applicable to the job.

> *A generic cover letter that has not been tailored to the position being applied for and the company being applied to will be disregarded.*
> Faiz Nazerali, Intellitech I.T. Solutions Ltd.

E-mail addresses can be tricky. I always recommend using a separate e-mail address for your job search. A typical teenager today opens an e-mail account between the ages of eight and fourteen. At that age, a person rarely creates an e-mail address that contains first name and surname. Young teenagers typically set up silly or funny e-mail addresses such as partyanimal@gmail.com, warrior@gmail.com, lordfireninja@gmail.com, and so on. While the young person grows up, all of his or her contacts and communications are saved within that same e-mail address created years earlier. Family and friends become accustomed to that specific e-mail address and will want to continue using it to contact the person. The former teenager, now a recent university graduate, applies for a job with that same silly e-mail address. What happens then? It may sound commonplace, but when a recruiter or hiring manager has to write an e-mail to an address like partyanimal@gmail.com, he or she will make assumptions about you and your character. They will certainly not be positive assumptions. Do you see my point? It's easy to create a new, more professional e-mail address for use in your job search. Always use the new and professional e-mail address for job applications; you should never use a silly e-mail address for job applications.

You should also avoid leaving long gaps in work history on a CV. Although you might have a gap in your work history for any number of legitimate reasons, not addressing it can send up red flags. If you have done a gap year, include it with a description of what you did. If you were pregnant or left work to care for an ill member of the family, this must be mentioned. You did additional studies? List them in the career section. Never just hope the gap will not be noticed. Add a clear, brief line about the gap. This mention could be as simple as "Left successful career to care for elderly parent for a year" or "Spent gap year traveling to India and Africa doing charity work with organization xyz."

Duncan Mathison, coauthor of *Unlock the Hidden Job Market: 6 Steps to a Successful Job Search When Times Are Tough*, highlights the importance of passing the *"So what, anybody can make that claim!"* test. He recommends leaving off the CV any generic claims or general statements not backed up by quantitative measures of achievement. With such a large volume of candidates applying for so few vacancies, it is important to stand out, states our anonymous recruiter interviewed in London. Standing out requires highlighting your strengths, skills, and achievements. But be careful not to stand out for the wrong reasons or to exaggerate—or worse, lie—in order to stand out.

> *Please avoid obvious exaggerations and lies. Yes, sometimes it does happen, and one can tell just from reading. Overestimated salary requirements when the experience does not match the price the candidate puts on himself. Lies and exxagerations are the major off-putting factors usually occurring during face-to-face communication.*
> *Julia Faida, Optimum Media OMD*

It is important not to stand out for the wrong reasons, such as "saying what they did not do or have not yet accomplished; applicants need to focus on what they have done or are in the process of achieving," (Amina Malik, Human Resource Manager, London). Do not claim to be a team leader but also able to work individually; state your preference. Do not claim to be a hard worker, because the term is overused. Yes, you do have to be a hard worker these days, because times have changed. The nine-to-five job no longer exists. In many cases you will work later, and you might have to work on weekends, constantly checking e-mail on your smartphone. We are all hard workers now. But what is a hard worker? I thought I was a hard worker until I met a few investment bankers with the ability (and the need) to work from 7:00 a.m. to 3:00 a.m. They are hard workers. But a hard worker is also a smart worker, a person who works normal hours but achieves twice as much as his or her peers. Instead of using overused words, refresh your application with a little search-and-replace exercise. Scan your CV for empty, overused words and phrases, such as outstanding, effective, strong, exceptional, good, excellent, driven, motivated, seasoned, energetic, and team player. "Watch out for words that are unsupported claims of greatness," says Mathison.

> *What puts me off in CVs is highlighting certain big words such as "strategist." Most of the time strategy is already done by someone else, and you are only copying them. People who really do it do not call themselves that. The candidate has to explain what value he or she brings to the organization.*
> *Cristiano Cardarelli, Contract Excellence Manager*

The nouns following those overused adjectives can be equally meaningless. Anyone who has ever had a coworker can claim to be a team player. "Do not say you are a good communicator or have excellent communication skills. Who doesn't have these?" asks Susan Ach, a career counselor at Marymount Manhattan College in New York City. Instead, list your accomplishments and let the hiring manager judge. If you are a good communicator, and you are applying for a sales job or a communications job, how can you explain your skill with facts? If you have successfully communicated with top executives, reached specific sales targets, and worked as account manager on a large number of accounts, then yes, you are a good professional. Awards or other forms of recognition can also be mentioned as evidence. Some words should be avoided, because they convey traits that employers consider standard for anybody who wants to be hired. You're motivated? Well, do you expect to be hired if you claim to be lazy or a slacker? Also on the no-no side are words that seek to overcome what you might think are your shortcomings. "Using 'seasoned' for 'over fifty' or 'energetic' for 'inexperienced' looks like spin and smells like spin," Mathison says. Keep the focus on what makes you right for the job. On the flip side, certain words can make hiring managers do a double-take in a positive sense. Light up their eyes with these ten words: created, increased, reduced, improved, developed, researched, accomplished, won, on time, and under budget. "We suggest that résumé writers include action words to describe their jobs," Ach says. Verbs project the image of someone who has the background and initiative to get things done. Employers can clearly comprehend what you have accomplished in the past and can use that as a basis for envisioning future success with their company. Think about it: If you were hiring, would you rather take on someone who calls herself a "productive manager" or someone who states that at her last job she "increased company profit by 3 percent, reduced the department's employee turnover to its lowest level in five years, and improved brand awareness by implementing a new social media strategy"? Finally, using verbs and nouns common to your specific industry can be beneficial. It shows your familiarity with the language of your field and optimizes your chances of getting past an automatic scan for key words. But remember, too, that all companies tend to speak a universal language: money. "Terms such as 'on time' and 'under budget' are often good. Hiring managers want to know you can get things done with minimum fuss," Mathison says.

I am not terribly interested in hobbies, but it is important to show your personality. Do not mention hobbies that will freak out your potential employer.

Sheryl Cusia, Boudicca Proxy

A key point is never to sound desperate on the CV or cover letter you circulate. Highlight immediately your skills and why you are keen to secure a role with that specific company. Make sure you capture the attention of the reader. "Unfortunately, some people will write what they have done in a very lengthy and uninteresting way, and by the time you are done reading that page of introduction you are already bored and ready to move on to the next candidate," states an anonymous financial recruiter in London.

Summary

1. If you do not have the ability to create a good CV, get somebody to do it for you. Make the investment.
2. The CV highlights your qualifications for employment in a particular job or career field. It is an individually designed summary of the person's personal, educational, and work experience qualifications as they relate to the employment sought.
3. A cover letter is a business letter that gives you the opportunity to introduce yourself to a prospective employer, express your interest in a position, and explain how you would add value to the organization.
4. Cover letters are becoming less and less important. Nonetheless, candidates should not miss the opportunity to write an outstanding cover letter that enables personality to shine outside the rigid structure of a CV.
5. Most of our experts believe that the CV must be between one and two pages depending on the level of the position: a one-page CV for people with less than five years of experience and a two-page CV once experience has increased.
6. The first half of the CV is the most important part. Candidates need to capture the recruiter's attention immediately, using facts and beginning each statement with an action word such as created, implemented, improved, or increased.

7. The recommended structure of a CV includes contact information; personal statement; employment history and accomplishments in reverse-chronological order; education; professional qualifications; certifications, accreditations, and professional memberships; awards and publications; computer and technical skills; and interests.

8. One of the most important parts of the CV is the personal statement, which is composed of a few sentences appearing at the top of the CV and is sometimes referred to as a career summary.

9. No longer than five lines, it must highlight key strengths, skills, and experience.

10. When reading CVs and cover letters, hiring managers and recruiters are put off by mistakes, bad formatting, excessive punctuation, and fancy colors. The CV and cover letter must be relevant to the position for which the candidate is applying and filled with interesting facts, skills, and achievements. Skills should be limited to those relevant to the relevant to the target job. It is also recommended to leave off the CV any generic claims or general statements not backed up by quantitative measures of achievement.

CHAPTER 3

The recruiting process, LinkedIn, and the role of headhunters

The recruiting process varies from organization to organization. Amina Malik describes it as a five-stage process involving business need assessment; candidate identification; candidate assessment and presentation; candidate interview, selection, and preparation of offer; and closure and follow-up.

1) **Business need assessment**
   a) *Define the objectives and specifications of the role. Is this a new role or a replacement? Has approval been received?*
   b) *Create the job title and description*
   c) *Develop a search plan and review of the business*

2) **Candidate identification**
   a) *Identify target sources*
   b) *Perform an extensive mapping of the organization and search the database for potential candidates, including*

internal ones who are looking for promotion or job change within the organization
  c) *Advertise the position internally (including a request for referrals from employees), with recruiting agencies, and more broadly outside the organization*
  d) *HR provides a status report to the hiring manager about the available CVs*

3) Candidate assessment and presentation
  a) *Screen and evaluate candidate résumés to create a short list*
  b) *HR/Headhunters discuss the short list with the business*
  c) *Conduct interviews with shortlisted candidates to assess skills, interest level, competency, and fit with the company's culture*
  d) *The candidates meet with an HR representation, the hiring manager, another member of the team, and the head of the business area*

4) Candidate interview, selection, and preparation of offer
  a) *Obtain feedback from all parties involved in the interview stage*
  b) *Participate in the decision-making process and provide inputs on the selected candidate's desired compensation*

5) Closure and follow-up
  a) *Check references*
  b) *Negotiate the offer, discuss job level and compensation, and obtain acceptance from the selected candidate*
  c) *Coordinate formalities of the onboarding process*
  d) *Conduct a closing review between HR and the business area to gauge the level of satisfaction with the process and the outcome*

The role of HR and its interaction with managers and recruiters will vary from company to company. The recruiting company may or may not be involved, depending on the size of the organization and the availability of the HR manager. The number of people internal to the company who are involved in the recruiting process may be one or several, depending on the role's importance and the future interaction that the candidate is expected to have with other departments. Across various industries and company sizes, though, we have found that the trend is for the hiring manager to be the final decision maker. Although networking with HR managers and recruiters is important, it is recommended to always prioritize the networking with the hiring manager.

> *The hiring manager tends to be in control from the onset, while the members of the HR team only work as mediators and ensure the hiring manager uses the right templates and so forth. But overall, the hiring manager is involved from the beginning after the online test has been passed.*
>
> Tosin Ojikutu, Investec

> *In our company HR and hiring managers do not usually work together much. The HR manager, in our case, checks the candidates' skills, such as foreign language knowledge and math, and then does the paperwork when making the offer. Often the candidate goes to the hiring manager directly.*
>
> Julia Faida, Optimum Media OMD

The role of technologies, LinkedIn, and other professional social networks

In a nutshell, technology is nowadays the main tool for job searching other than networking. Today's job seekers have plenty of recruiting websites and search engines available to investigate a sector or market for relevant job opportunities. Finding jobs is not sufficient, though. Job seekers also have to be visible in order to themselves be found by potential employers. LinkedIn[5] is now one of the most important

5 LinkedIn was cofounded by Reid Hoffman, a former executive vice president in charge of business and corporate development at PayPal. The website, launched in May

means of finding jobs. It is a social-networking service designed specifically for the business community and used by individuals for professional networking, connecting, and job searching. Companies and recruiters use LinkedIn for recruiting and for providing company information to prospective employees. LinkedIn members can search for jobs, join groups, research companies, and network with other people. Companies can post information and job listings on their pages. Companies can also contact LinkedIn members for recruiting purposes. The goal of the LinkedIn website is to allow registered members to establish and manage networks of people they know and trust professionally. A LinkedIn member's profile page, which emphasizes employment history and education, has professional network news feeds and a limited number of customizable modules. Basic membership for LinkedIn is free. Members of a person's network members are called connections. Unlike other free social networking sites like Facebook and Twitter, LinkedIn requires connections to have a preexisting relationship with each other. With a basic membership, a person can establish connections only with someone he or she has worked with, knows professionally (online or offline), or has gone to school with.

If you are reading this book and do not yet have a LinkedIn profile, please go to the website (http://www.linkedin.com) and create an account for yourself. "The demand for jobs is so high that LinkedIn has become [the] same as a telephone. You have the ability to contact anyone, and it can really work" (Antonio Iandolo, DB Apparel).

Our company is very open to candidates approaching us via LinkedIn directly. We as a company are also using LinkedIn effectively to get our message(s) out.

Michael Witte, Capgemini

The main change is around the importance of LinkedIn and the influence and information your virtual network can give you. People know that sending a CV will not ensure a

2003, currently has more than 300 million members from two hundred countries and 170 industries. According to Reid Hoffman, 27 percent of LinkedIn subscribers are recruiters.

response. You can be approached or find a suitable role by just having a profile listed and finding someone you have worked with before who now works at a company of interest to you—that is the best possible reference you can get, and they will also understand the hiring process. LinkedIn, more than any other networking tool, is very important both as a student and experienced hire.

Victoria Barry-Woods, Allegis Group

I applied for my role via LinkedIn, and my company advertises all roles on LinkedIn.

Daniel Singham, Toluna

The social network changed the recruiting process. I am often approached by headhunters via Facebook and LinkedIn. Therefore, it is always the case that you should maintain a decent social profile.

Julia Faida, Optimum Media

Now that you have created a LinkedIn account, you need to fill in your profile page. Do not leave your profile page empty, but do not fill it in quickly with random information either. Start your profile by writing a personal message that is a concise description of your main skills and experience. "In a bad economy, people just want the candidates for the money they can invest. So technologies need to help candidates make their CVs look as good as possible, focus on results," states Kelly Blokdijk of Talent Talks. "LinkedIn will allow you to approach managers directly, but then you will need to stand out" (Pritul Khagram, People Force International). When on LinkedIn, look at various networks, job boards, and how professionals in your sector have set up their profiles. Put together a well-constructed, well-written profile for yourself. You should not list a lot of skills or things done in your previous jobs. The profile has to be concise and straight to the point. List your former and current coworkers, partners, and other colleagues. Use the right key words. Your profile page must represent you, your education (if you are relatively young), your work experience, and your main skills. These skills need to be endorsed by members of your network, because the more endorsements you receive the more appealing your profile will be. The key words used are very important because they will also help you to be noticed. A recruiter or HR representative looking for candidates will type key words into LinkedIn, and LinkedIn's algorithms will provide a list candidates who have those skills. Search for various jobs that interest you, and then use those key words in your profile. Connect with the right people in your sector of interest. I specifically recommend trying to get recommendations from people who can confirm your abilities and skills. Getting recommendations can be challenging, and asking for it is tricky. When a person is seen working on his or her LinkedIn profile, colleagues or friends will immediately think he or she is in the process of looking for work. When asking for a recommendation, if someone asks whether you are in the process of looking for a different job, just say no. I recommend being vague and suggesting that you are updating your profile because it will help your credibility in dealing with existing clients of your current company; you are good and you want people to know this. Also, do not forget to "follow" companies for which you might want to work, because this will automatically help you in receiving their job postings and getting noticed by them.

> *LinkedIn has tools for connecting. Unfortunately, 80 percent of people do not have the good taste to write a nice, personal message. Those people are out. If you do not know how to build the right relationship, this is not the right world for you. High-level and important people receive five or ten requests to connect on LinkedIn per month, but they often ignore them because the people sending the requests are not highly ranked enough. Besides, when linking with somebody, you should specify who you are and what you want to do. Building contacts requires time, and you need to have the right etiquette to keep your network. Connecting with the wrong person can bring your network down. There are indeed companies who approach a person, a candidate, via LinkedIn*

especially when launching a new product line or entering a new market. They need new blood and will look for it via LinkedIn. Obviously, LinkedIn is a level below a living network, because you have to trust what is written. Networking is the most important, networking guarantees survival.
Cristiano Cardarelli, Contract Excellence Manager

Despite LinkedIn being probably the most famous social network for professionals, there are a few other websites worth mentioning:

- **Xing**, a European business network with more than 7 million members;
- **Biznik,** a community of entrepreneurs and small businesses dedicated to helping each other succeed;
- **Cmypitch,** a business website for UK entrepreneurs to get quotes, advice, and more;
- **Cofoundr,** a community for entrepreneurs, programmers, designers, investors, and other individuals involved with starting new ventures;
- **EFactor,** an online community and virtual marketplace designed for entrepreneurs by entrepreneurs;
- **Networking for Professionals,** a business network that combines online networking and real-life events;
- **Ryze,** a business networking community that allows users to organize themselves by interests, location, and current and past employers; and
- **Facebook,** an online social networking service used for any type of social interaction, including job search.

The role of headhunters

Recruiters are important as well, so present yourself well; the recruiter is the eye and the ears of the company. It is a big mistake to think the recruiter doesn't matter during the recruiting process. There are always people better out there.

If you ask yourself what you should wear, always dress more formally than you think you should. Go overdressed.
                    Julia Barber, Cornell Partnership

The role of recruiting companies varies by industry and the seniority of the position sought. Several respondents to our survey confirmed that they prefer to utilize recruiting companies when recruiting for mid- to senior-level positions. For such positions, the recruiter will conduct a sort of investigation of the possible candidates currently employed by competitors, professionals who have relevant experience and might be looking for new opportunities. It is very important to prepare for an interview with a recruiter as if he or she were the hiring manager. First, the recruiter will only forward to the company the applications of the best candidates and best matches for the position. The recruiter is not there to help candidates find a job. The recruiter has clients (firms with vacancies to fill) that will only pay a commission to the recruiter if he or she finds the best match for the job. Because the recruiter works for commission, the higher the position's salary the higher the commission. Keep this in mind if you have just graduated from university and are looking for a position with a low salary, because the recruiter will be less likely to help you compared to when you have few years of experience and can command a higher salary. Also, keep in mind that recruiters are not there to help job seekers change careers or find them jobs that are only a 50 percent match to their current skill set.

Recruiters will call you if you have the right CV. You need to have certain skills to be called. Your CV has to be relevant; there is no point for recruiters to speak to the wrong person.
          Anonymous financial recruiter, London, United Kingdom

In addition, candidates sometimes think that recruiters are not important during the process and do not attend the interview impeccably dressed. According to Julia Barber (Cornell Partnership), this is wrong. "Recruiters are important, so candidates should presented themselves well; the recruiter is the eyes and ears of the company. It is a big mistake to think the recruiter doesn't matter during the recruiting process. There are always people better out there. If you ask yourself what you should wear, always dress more formally than you think you should. Go overdressed."

Everyone speaks about the hidden job market, but we often forget the role of recruiting companies. "The recruiting industry is big, almost as big as the real estate sector in London. There are lots of recruiters, because there is demand. I believe there are lots of jobs but not enough good candidates with the right skills," states Cristiano Cardarelli, Contract Excellence Manager. The recruiting industry is based on the goal of providing candidates to a client company for a price based on a job specification advertised by the client. Recruiting agencies are paid only if they deliver the right candidate who is hired and remains at the client company beyond an agreed-upon probationary period. The recruiter usually investigates the market for candidates who are currently working within the same industry and country as the client company. The recruiter's role depends on his or her level of authority but mostly on his or her ability to interview candidates effectively and choose wisely among those candidates.

Our experts have also described the importance of recruiters in the context of poaching from competition. Often, in the market a company will include a noncompete clause in an employee's contract. Noncompete clauses are a gray area of employment law in various countries and are rarely enforceable. A typical noncompete clause is intended to prevent the employee from working for a specified list of competitors for a certain period after leaving the current company, usually six to twelve months. My suggestion: never let noncompete clauses scare you or refrain you from trying to move on with your career and maybe move to a competitor. Most non competes are in fact too broad or unnecessary. The employer often creates unnecessary restrictions on its employees and courts will not uphold the non-competition clauses, especially if they forbid the employee from finding work with a competitor in the entire state for a certain period. You need to earn a living after all and most likely you will do by using your best skills. When a company is interested in hiring a senior manager or director from a competitor, HR will often retain a headhunter to investigate the market to find talent or specifically poach one person. Recruiters are usually engaged in at least one of the following phases:

- Confirmation of candidate interest
- Screening candidates for qualifications
- Recommendations to client
- Organization of final interviews
- Selection of the desired candidate

Confirmation of candidate interest

An initial telephone screening is the earliest stage in the interview process, and the recruiter's role in it is twofold. After you apply for a job (usually via e-mail), your CV will be screened and assessed. If you have the right skills, you will usually receive a telephone interview to screen whether your work history and experience is consistent with the job's requirements. Many recruiters will start the telephone interview by describing the job and then will ask if the candidate is still interested. They then follow up with questions about your work experience and qualifications to see if you meet the basic requirements of the job.

Screening candidates for qualifications

Generally speaking, the recruiter's role is to present potential candidates to hiring managers and HR representatives after having determined that they are qualified for the position. After the 2008 financial crisis, many industries have become niches, with very few specialised players and market experts. For this reason, recruiters can easily spot whether the candidate is qualified for a position. The recruiter will ask certain questions and observe the way a candidate describes his or her qualifications. For example, recruiters ask behavioral interview questions to gauge whether management candidates really understand the basic principles of how to lead departmental functions and manage employees. A typical behavioral interview question is, "Tell me about a time when you had to delegate an important assignment to an employee whose performance had been declining." From this type of question, the recruiter can gauge whether you understand how to prioritize departmental responsibilities and how you handle employee issues. The recruiter will also receive guidance from clients about the existing team's profile and will evaluate whether the candidate would be a good fit with the existing team. "If, for example, I am recruiting for a client who has a team made up of people in their twenties, I will most likely exclude from selection all candidates who are not recent graduates. We can see if the candidate is on the way up or on the way down. What I mean is that, if there is a person who has thirty years of experience and went to school In the '80s and the '70s, I know there are certain clients out there who will be interested in that profile, but some other clients will just not want to hire this person; the person has already done the job, so will not be able to come in and be flexible and understand dynamics that might have changed. It is not prejudice, it is not ageist, is it just what clients want because of team dynamics" (Anonymous recruiter, London, United Kingdom). A manager also needs to look at what is best for the team and the company in terms of stability. If a candidate has held very senior positions for years but then has been out of work for some months due to redundancy, he or she may accept any job. Bearing in mind that a client will expect to recruit a person and then retain him or her for the long run, however, will the hiring manager consider such a candidate? Most likely not. Again, it is not discrimination; it is just how the market is and thinks. If the person has been senior and earned very good money, how long will he or she last being managed by a younger person? How happy will the candidate be, knowing he or she earned much more money in the past? The interviewer will want to ascertain clearly whether a person applying for a lower-paid job really wants to take a pay cut (maybe in exchange for a less stressful job or the ability to work from home) or is only taking it because of unfortunate circumstances and lack of better opportunities.

Recommendations to client

Recruiters play an essential role in making recommendations to hiring managers. Through the questions they ask candidates early in the interview process, recruiters compare candidates' qualifications and rank the candidates from the most qualified down to the candidate whose qualifications are average. The recruiter then meets with the hiring manager, typically in a face-to-face interview, to explain why each candidate has been selected.

Organization of final interviews

For some panel interviews, the recruiter is responsible for organizing or selecting panel members, coordinating some of the interview logistics, and providing the panel members with appropriate interview questions. The recruiter may also participate in the panel interview to ensure it runs on schedule. After the panel finishes asking questions, the recruiter (or an external recruiting consultant) collects notes from the panel members and may even tally the responses to recommend a final candidate.

Selection of the desired candidate

When all candidates have undergone a second or third round of interviews, the recruiter's job is not yet over. During this final stage in the interview process, the recruiter listens to feedback from the hiring manager and checks references for the top candidates. The recruiter will draft suitable questions to ask each candidate's references and determine which candidate is best suited for the job based on the hiring manager's preference and information obtained from the references.

Summary

1. The recruitment process can be described as a five-stage process involving business need assessment; candidate identification; candidate assessment and presentation; candidate interview, selection, and preparation of offer; and closure and follow-up.
2. The role of HR and its interaction with managers and recruiters will vary from company to company. In most cases, the hiring manager will be the decision maker.
3. Besides in-person networking, technology is now the main tool for job searching. LinkedIn is the most famous and important social networking service designed for the business community, used by individuals for professional networking, connecting, and job searching. Every job seeker should have an updated LinkedIn profile.
4. A LinkedIn profile should represent the candidate, his or her education, work experience, and main skills; it should begin with a concise description of the person's main skills and experience.
5. Recruiters are also very important in the recruitment process, but unfortunately not many people understand this. Candidates should prepare and present themselves well even when meeting with a recruiter.
6. The role of recruiting companies varies by industry, and recruiters become extremely important when recruiting for mid- to senior-level positions. Recruiters will only call candidates who have the right CV and skills; there is no point for a recruiter to speak to the wrong person.
7. The recruiter's role depends on his or her level of authority but mostly on his or her ability to interview candidates effectively and choose wisely among those candidates. Most recruiters are involved in the interview process from preliminary screening

to selecting candidates who are qualified to fill the position, while the hiring manager will conduct the final interview and complete the recruiting process.

8. Because the final decision maker is always the hiring manager rather than the recruiter or HR representative, the candidate should try as much as possible to directly approach the hiring manager.

CHAPTER 4

Networking is the key!

Networking is incredibly important! You make business for yourself by networking. Being part of a certain group of interests, business clubs, or societies is important because it opens your mind to opportunities. A person living abroad could use the societies of his or her country or city. You need to build a strong network; make sure your network remembers you for being amazing! A lot of graduates are scared of networking. They lack the confidence, and they will not even know how to network unless they go to a top university.

Sheryl Cusia, Boudicca Proxy

Build your network and use it wisely...

Paolo Garonna, Federazione Banche Italiane

What is networking? Wikipedia defines networking as a "socioeconomic business activity by which groups of like-minded businesspeople recognize, create, or act upon business opportunities." Networking is important in many areas and can help find clients, business partners, employers, and so forth. In the context of the job search, I would define networking as an activity that helps people with a certain industry interest and skill set to connect with managers and recruiters within that industry. The connections found via networking help people with a certain industry interest and skill set to either gather industry knowledge or find work opportunities.

Surveys in various countries indicate that about a third of workers find jobs through word of mouth. The table below, based on a 2003 UK survey (the most recent UK information available[6]), seems to confirm the trend.

Method	Men (%)	Women (%)
Reply to an advertisement	24.2	31.6
Hearing from someone who worked there (networking)	31.7	25.8
Direct application	14.1	15.6
Private employment agency	10.3	9.4
Job center	9.0	7.3
Some other way	10.7	10.3

Many jobs are not advertised at all. Others are advertised only within a small network of individuals who have restricted access. Based on the answers received during my interviews, most interviewees have confirmed that networking has become incredibly important in the years since the 2008 crisis. About 90 percent of the respondents to the interviews conducted for this book stated that networking is the most effective way to find a job. All respondents mentioned networking as one of the ways to find a job. Due to the scarcity of jobs, people who are more visible via networking have much better chances of finding work.

The network is extremely important. An individual is only as efficient in finding business opportunities as the network he has. If you do not have a network, you are nobody. You are in danger if your network is only in your company or your sector.
Cristiano Cardarelli, Contract Excellence Manager

6   John Lees, *How to Get a Job You'll Love* (Maidenhead, UK: McGraw-Hill Professional, 2012).

There are two types of networking. The first one is for maintaining connection with your existing contacts, and the second is for establishing new contacts.

The most important aspect of networking is to keep the network alive. You need to work hard at it. It's a simple formula: keep connected + reconnect = a strong network.

Depending on where you are in your career, reconnecting may mean contacting professors, university advisers, and internship supervisors, or it may mean getting in touch with former colleagues, managers, and business acquaintances. Find them, e-mail them, and call them. Ask them out for coffee. Ask how they are (networking is social, after all), and let them know the specifics of your job search (industry, location, and so forth). Ask if they know of anything or anyone. Recently, a friend and former work colleague whom I hadn't spoken with in two years reached out to me looking for work at the exact time when my firm was recruiting…and she got the job!

Now that you have reached out to your existing contacts, even more important is that you follow up! Everyone is busy in our society; someone not having replied to you does not mean there is no opportunity. Pushing your contacts hard can be the most efficient way of getting a job. Pick up the phone and give them a call!

If, however, you are at a temporary dead end with your current contacts, you need to find new ones. It is as simple as that. This is sometimes called speed networking. Go to networking events sponsored by your university, industry, city, and so on. Look beyond traditional networking events. Consider going to lectures, neighborhood council meetings, community bar crawls (but go easy on the sauce and the drinks!). Each of these provides an opportunity to meet people with similar interests, and you can have fun in the process. Meet people, speak to people. Every person you speak to can potentially become important in your life and find you a job, either directly or indirectly.

The responses received from my panel of interviewees have provided strong evidence that currently over half of jobs are filled via referrals or networking. Tosin Ojikutu of Investec states that, in his personal experience, "hiring managers already know who they wish to employ, and the recruitment process is simply a form-filling exercise via mean of one manager's existing network of contacts." Daniel Singham of Toluna says that "networking is the key, because at the end of the day most people know how to write a good CV, how to impress in an interview, but the key is having recommendations. This gives more backup." Why is networking such an important aspect of the job search? Mishelle Sassun explains that "nobody wants to recommend mediocre people, and so people only send through recommendations for candidates who are believed to be a really good fit for the job. People recommend candidates they know really well from either studying together or working together at other companies. It brings insights that are really difficult to judge in regular interviews." Many companies have established referral programs that encourage employees to refer candidates to their employer. The company will pay its employees a fee for referrals, and these fees increase based on the seniority of the position being hired. According to Kelly Blokdijk of Talent Talks, "people hire via networking because it is good to know or have an idea about who they are about to employ, either directly or through other connections." It is a matter of company culture. Bottom line, if an employee recommends someone he or she knows, the person will likely fit into the company.

Networking is extremely important in the current market. It is not about what you know...but "who" you know. Therefore, we would more likely hire someone through our network connections than someone who simply applied for a position (through their CV). So far, I'd say our hiring rate of network referrals as opposed to direct applications would be 90 percent network referrals.
        Faiz Nazerali, Intellitech I.T. Solutions Ltd.

Networking has become a very important tool in any industry; it is about who you know and not what you know! Senior hires, in particular, tend to come through referrals. Networking with people in their industry, attending seminars and events, and using social media to its fullest capacity are all approaches

people should be using while looking for a job. I find LinkedIn, in particular, to be a brilliant networking tool.
Amina Malik, Human Resource Manager, London

Networking is important, of course, but in most cases not for entry-level positions. I would say it mostly works best for middle to higher management positions.
Julia Faida, Optimum Media

How do we get started in becoming great networkers? Start with your existing network. Remember, keep connected + reconnect = a strong network. Start with people you know, and then, once your existing network is exhausted, move on to those you don't know.

Prepare your elevator speech or TMAY

The concept of an "elevator speech" or tell me about yourself (TMAY) refers to a twenty- to sixty-second speech or statement that briefly and memorably introduces you to other people. In such a small amount of time you need to be able to spotlight your skills and accomplishments, focusing on the benefits you can provide to others, particularly prospective employers. Depending on your circumstances, your elevator speech can finish by hinting that you are looking for a job. This can prompt the other person to consider you for opportunities, and you can then follow up with him or her after the meeting.

Keep business cards available

Business cards are your passports to networking. Whether you are looking for work or you are already employed, how can you ensure the person in front of you will remember your name or write down your mobile number or e-mail address? A business card must provide contact information and a brief description of what you do. You can find inexpensive business card services online. Always carry some business cards with you. When you meet people, ask to trade business cards. Then you will have their contact information to use in networking. If they don't have cards, write their contact information on the back of your card. Be sure to note when you met them.

Interest yourself in what others say

When talking to other people, especially potential new contacts, you must be a good listener. Your networking conversations should be two-way interactions, not monologues you deliver. Show an interest in the new people you meet. Learn about their contacts and employers, and try to direct your conversation toward a useful common ground. Make the conversation meaningful. If someone talks about a current activity, offer to help. Even when people are willing to help you, they will also be interested in how you can help them. Networking is about mutual support, not just other people doing you favors. Stay alert for opportunities to help others. Everyone will be amazed to hear you are willing to help. They will remember, and later they might return the favor.

Be organized and effective when contacting your network

Periodically contact some members of your network to catch up on anything you believe is relevant to that specific relationship. You could share an interesting article, invite them to attend a networking event with you, ask them for information about a person in their network, and so on. But make sure you know what you want to say before you pick up the telephone. Make a list of points you want to make or questions you want to ask. Keep this list in front of you while on the telephone or sending an e-mail. Telephoning is usually more effective.

Always use discretion

Don't contact the members of your network too frequently, or they may feel you are stalking them. Every three or four weeks is about right, unless you have something very specific to discuss. Make sure the person you are contacting knows you and remembers you and that you have something in common, whether a connection or mutual interest.

Networking ideas

An interesting book I recommend regarding the topics of job search, career change, and networking is *How to Get a Job You'll Love* (2013–2014 edition). The author, John Lees, specializes in helping people make difficult decisions—difficult because they don't know what to do next or because there are barriers in the way of success. Lees's book, together with the responses from my panel of interviewees, gave me a list of activities for a creative networking job search:

- Identify all likely employers and useful agencies in your sector or field of interest by scrutinizing job advertisements, LinkedIn, and career websites, and approach these companies directly on a speculative basis.
- Talk to recruitment consultants who regularly advertise jobs in your sector.
- Attend all free (or low-cost) seminars and conferences in your sector of interest.
- Conduct informational interviews to deepen your understanding of a sector.
- Ask for meetings with decision makers who are hubs of strong networks.
- Maintain a strong online presence through appropriate use of social media.

- A person living abroad could use clubs, groups, or country societies (e.g., the Italian society in London) in his or her city. For example, I attend meetings at the Italian embassy in London to connect with key Italian decision makers.
- Join the alumni network of the university at which you studied.
- Undertake temporary or project work that increases your visibility to decision makers.
- Hang around the pubs where key decision makers with whom you want to connect tend to hang out. For example, a person I know was interested in a career in trading and got a job by frequenting a pub where bankers of a famous bank gathered after work.
- Speak to your clients. If you are seeking a career change, your client might already think highly of you and be happy to hire you or consider you as a partner or consultant.

Summary

1. Many jobs are not advertised at all. Others are advertised only within a small network of individuals who have restricted access. Networking has become incredibly important in the years since the 2008 crisis. There is strong evidence that over half of jobs now are filled via referrals or networking.
2. All of the respondents mentioned networking as one of the ways to find a job. Due to the scarcity of jobs, people who are more visible via networking have much better chances of finding work.
3. There are two types of networking. The first one is for maintaining connection with your existing contacts and the second is for establishing new contacts.
4. Reconnecting with existing contacts may mean contacting professors, university advisers, and internship supervisors, or it may mean getting in touch with former colleagues, managers, and business acquaintances.

5. If your existing contacts are not useful, you need to find new ones. Meeting people is the key. Every person you speak to can potentially become important in your life and find you a job, either directly or indirectly.
6. To become great networkers, job seekers should: prepare an elevator speech, keep business cards available and hand them out to new contacts, show interest in what other people say and engage with them, offer to help others in their activities, be organized and effective when contacting members of their network, and use discretion.
7. Activities that will lead to creative networking include: identifying all likely employers and useful agencies in your sector or field of interest and approaching those companies directly, attending free (or low-cost) seminars and conferences in your sector of interest, conducting informational interviews to deepen your understanding of a sector, asking for meetings with decision makers who are hubs of strong networks, maintaining a strong online presence through appropriate use of social media, joining the alumni network of the university at which you studied, undertaking temporary or project work that increases your visibility to decision makers, and hanging around the pubs where decision makers with whom you want to connect tend to hang out.

CHAPTER 5

How to impress during an interview

Imagine this. You have just arrived at the office of the company for which you hope to work. You have made it on time for the interview. You wait ten or fifteen minutes to be called in for the interview. Most likely your tension rises, and you begin to sweat. After a short time, the office administrator will introduce you to the person who will interview you. This is what happens at that time:

1. Seconds 1 and 2—The manager observes you, your appearance, and your clothing. "Dress code is important. Do not give the interviewers reasons to get distracted. Do not wear anything excessive; women should not wear too much makeup, men should keep ties quiet." (Julia Barber, Cornell Partnership) "Did the applicant shave prior to the interview? Did the applicant wear a dress/skirt/slacks or suit? Would I feel comfortable with this person representing our organization?" asks Michael O'Brien (BNY Mellon). The candidate should be well-groomed and look professional.
2. Seconds 3 to 5—You follow the manager into an interview room. When you accidentally hit a chair, the manager thinks you are nervous.

3. Seconds 6 to 15—You have your first conversation, usually not related to the position for which you are interviewing. This is just a chat, maybe about the weather, your journey to attend the interview, the beauty of the offices, or how busy the manager is. Are you at ease? Often, these ten seconds are extremely important because the manager will decide if he or she will enjoy working with you on a personal level.

4. Seconds 16 to 30—The manager thinks about the ice-breaker conversation you just had and your answers. The manager may know exactly what questions he or she will be asking you or may have shown up without having read your CV or having forgotten who you are and the purpose of the interview. Based on a gut feeling, the manager will decide whether to give you an easy interview, an average interview, or a difficult interview. While considering that, the manager may start smelling something. It is your perfume. How pleasant, or worse, how strong is it? Does he or she like it? Yes. Is that good? Not yet. This manager leads a team of ten, and the candidate will sit next to two people and face three more. Will all of those people like the smell? A manager must consider them as well. The manager certainly does not want to hire a candidate who does not know how to dose his or her cologne. Too much cologne or no cologne (or no deodorant) at all could frustrate colleagues and compromise their productivity. Does a manager want to risk this? And if the candidate rises in the ranks, will the manager send him or her to a client meeting knowing the smell might irritate the client or prospective client?

The situation just described has been intentionally exaggerated to show how many things can happen in the very beginning of an interview. One interview can change your life: it can lead to a dream job or just secure a salary that will help you get by. Yet so many people get it wrong. Based on the responses received for this book as well as my years of experience conducting job interviews, I have identified a number of issues that can negatively affect the interview process.

Don't be unprepared; know the company

One of the first questions you will be asked at an interviews is, "Do you know our company?" The Internet enables you to prepare yourself very well; going into an interview completely unprepared is just not good. Never go into an interview without having researched the industry, the company, the manager, and as much as you can about the specific position. "Knowing the company, concentrating on the right answers and on what the company needs is paramount," summarizes Pritul Khagram. Do not tell the interviewer you have come to learn about the company, because that will turn them off. You need to be knowledgeable and find out in advance everything you can about the company for which you want to work. Preparation shows that you are serious about what you want and that you want the position for which you are interviewing. "The candidate needs to demonstrate he or she knows the company and the position he or she is interviewing for. People who come unprepared do not demonstrate sufficient effort to warrant further consideration," states Michael O'Brien of BNY Mellon.

The first impression

Research shows that for many jobs, creating a positive first impression is fundamental. The first thirty seconds of an interview play a critical role toward receiving a job offer. Across all interviews conducted for this book, the concept of making a good first impression was highlighted by all respondents.

> *First impression is always the most important.*
> *Antonio Iandolo, DB Apparel*

"Start with a firm handshake," states Daniel Singham of Toluna. This will show confidence. Try to not have sweaty hands—keep a paper tissue in your pocket or use a little talcum powder just before entering the company's office. "It is scary for a manager to see candidates who go to an interview shaking, super-stressed, and emotional; it is a bad sign of being unable to work under stress," says Mishelle Sassun of Bee Creations. "Very often the hiring manager will make his first judgment call within the first thirty seconds," declares Pritul Khagram of People Force International. According to Amina Malik (Human Resourcr Manager, London), you should consider the following to give a good first impression:

- A firm handshake,
- Eye contact,
- Smart, polished shoes with closed toes,
- Minimum jewelry,
- Clean, short nails, and
- Tidy hair, possibly short if you are a man.

"Visual presentation and appearance is also important. Do not give the interviewers reasons to get distracted. Do not wear anything excessive; women should not wear too much makeup; men should keep ties quiet," states Julia Barber of Cornell Partnership. Of the same opinion is Cindy Anastasi of CCBill EU: "I want to see the person looking clean and smart, shaved, if [the person has] long hair [it should be] well taken care of. Presenting oneself as being well groomed (the way the person is dressed, their posture, and so forth) is fundamental across all industries. It contributes to making a positive first impression, which is crucial. Remember, it is not like going to a movie, this is a business meeting. Any fragrance that is too strong, a damp, weak handshake, the an inability to maintain eye contact, or giving wishy-washy answers, can immediately give the wrong impression. Do not pretend to know an answer if you do not. Unfortunately, many of the answers we get are very superficial, which indicates that the interviewee doesn't have a sound grasp of the fundamentals of the job at hand. 'Will this person fit on my team? Will he or she get along with colleagues and be a good fit for the company?' These are the bottom-line questions a manager wants to gauge."

Being late

The first impression is actually created even before the interview begins, even before the candidate meets the hiring manager or recruiter. "The candidate will start by being on time, but not too early," states Michael Witte of Capgemini. "I have sent candidates home for being five minutes late. There is no excuse for being late for a job interview, ever...unless you contacted the hiring manager, while en route, and explained the reason for being late," he concludes. I could not agree more. Recently a candidate arrived with a 40mins delay for an interview telling me he was late because he could not find a cab. At the same time, it would have taken him 20mins to get to my workplace from his home if he had come by underground. Do not take the risk to be late, study your route before the interview!

Confirming the positive first impression

Now that you have successfully passed the first thirty seconds of an interview, what happens next? The candidate must confirm the positive first impression.

> *There are certain things that can put off the hiring manager— for example, falling, bumping the chair when you arrive, entering the interviewer's personal space, taking his or her papers, etc.*
> Stefano Bottaro, Opera Theatre of Rome

> *Being friendly, professional, honest, open, and relaxed will create a great first impression. Be precise about what you want and about your experiences. A hiring manager is put off by the incompatibility of ambitions to skills and expertise,*

aggressiveness that can be the case when the candidate cannot answer certain questions or suspects being criticized. Too much nervousness can also be quite an issue.

Julia Faida, Optimum Media OMD

Julia Barber of Cornell Partnership says, "In the United Kingdom, Europe, and North America, face to face is all about eye contact,[7] well-constructed sentences, listening well to the questions, being articulate and answering questions well, and doing a nice presentation if needed. It is difficult to pull back a bad first impression." Confidence and self-awareness are two additional factors that are crucial during an interview. Faiz Nazerali of Intellitech I.T. Solutions Ltd. states that "confidence in the candidate to be able to hold a dialogue with the interviewer as well as being conversant with information supplied in their CV and cover letter will create a great first impression." Sheryl Cusia of Boudicca Proxy reinforces the message: "You need to be on. You exist, but you are not present. If you are interviewing you need to be on. Eye contact, listening, and smiling are fundamental. Candidates may be impressive with their experience and CVs, but if they are not on they will not get the job."

Know your experience and describe it

Despite the recession, a lot of people we are interviewing are not up to scratch. You get these fantastic CVs, but then you realize the candidate has no clue. If you put something on a CV, expect to be asked about it, and you should know about it.

Cindy Anastasi, CCBill EU

---

7   On the other hand, only sporadic or brief eye contact is considered acceptable in some other cultures, especially in Asia. For example, in China and Japan children show respect to their elders by not making intense eye contact, employees do not make eye contact with employers, students do not force eye contact with teachers, and so on. The rule of thumb in Asian, African, and Latin American cultures is to be careful about making eye contact with anyone who could be seen as a social or professional superior.

If you are going to an interview, you need to know why you are there and who you are applying to work for. Researching the company is a must. "The interviewee has to be well prepared," states Angelo Chirulli, LEXeFISCAL. "A great put-off is memorizing the entire CV. This is certainly a very big no-no!" (Faiz Nazerali, Intellitech I.T. Solutions Ltd.). "A person who is not well researched and prepared will put off the hiring manager. If an interviewee doesn't know why he or she wants to work for an organization, how can they prove genuine passion and interest? Remember all the time that the person interviewing you could instead be doing something more valuable," argues Victoria Barry-Woods of Allegis Group.

> *I test the knowledge against the CV. I ask indirect questions that you should be able to master based on the knowledge you are telling me about in your CV.*
> *Cristiano Cardarelli, Contract Excellence Manager*

Do not overuse expressions

We have all heard expressions such as "I am a problem solver" or "I am a team player." General descriptions of how great you are will not help you impress the interviewer unless you add specific examples of your success. You should also be careful of descriptions that can become double-edged statements. If you say "I am a perfectionist," that could be great for some jobs but very bad for others. If a manager needs quick results, he or she will often not need or even want a perfectionist; instead, the manager will need a pragmatic person.

Do not criticize or complain about your current employer

Although you may be unhappy at your current company, your interviewer doesn't need to hear about it. First, you will not get a job out of mercy. The interviewer will not decide to employ you because you feel miserable in your current job. Second, be professional and try not to disclose confidential information, because it will show that you might do the same to the new company you want to join. The bottom line is that if you speak negatively about your current employer, chances are that you will speak negatively about your new employer at some point. Never bring any trash talk from your job into the interview. The best way to tell your interviewer about your unhappiness could be by indirectly stating that you do not always agree with your employer's decisions or that you do not always see eye to eye with your manager. Such an explanation could actually show that you can think for yourself, especially if you can quote a specific positive example. But remember: never trash-talk anyone.

Do not talk money during the first interview, unless asked

Another important factor in recruiting is remuneration. Your compensation package is a matter for major discussion. Over the past seven years I have conducted hundreds of job interviews, and in most of them, the compensation offered by the company or requested by the candidate played a very important role. Not long ago I interviewed a candidate who spent a third of the interview talking about how much money he was currently making and how his lifestyle was linked to his current salary: from an expensive house in West London, to the new car he had just bought, to his last vacation in Australia. He was a brilliant candidate who had excellent experience, a strong CV, and impressive knowledge of the industry. Did I hire him? No. In fact, I did not even make him an offer. Why? First, I was distracted by his comments about money and so I could not focus enough on his experience. Second, I thought that he was so focused on money that he would cause issues in the long term, maybe by being too demanding during an annual review. Self-absorbed people, too eager and not able to listen to or interact with the interviewer usually tend to be disregarded and not considered for a second round of interviews. You can talk about money with a recruiter because he or she needs to put you in the right position for the right money; however, try not to talk about money during the first interview with a hiring manager. If you are asked about money, just provide some guidance. Managers know that good candidates cost more money, but it is better to let them come up with the right offer after having realized how good you are and how valuable your experience and skills are. If they understand you are amazing, then they will also be able to speak to a superior about how good you are and explain why you deserve maybe more money than the original job was intended to pay. If the manager thinks during the early stages of an interview that you are too expensive, he or she will not even listen to what else you say.

Ask questions

In most job interviews the first twenty minutes will be entirely focused on yourself and your experience. At some point, the interviewer will usually stop asking questions and will start presenting the position. After that explanation, usually you will be asked whether you have any questions about the job or the company. Do not just answer negatively, do not just state that everything is clear. The research you have done about the company may have uncovered facts that you can ask about, or you may want to know about the scope for personal development. Be careful, though, because this is a dangerous area. Small to medium-sized companies may hire you to do a role that has no scope for personal development. At times—and this is unfortunate—too much ambition is not seen positively by employers. You may also wish to get more information about the role or the company's culture. You will probably have loads of questions as soon as you walk out of the interview, so it is better to ask some right now. Managers like inquisitive people, people who think for themselves and want to learn. Additionally, candidates who ask no questions are seen by many managers as people who will accept any job and who do not have a clear understanding of the position they have applied for. Instead, consult your interviewer on the job and try to show understanding of the role by hinting at experience or skills you have that could be helpful for the company.

Have an incisive closure

Wrapping up the interview is also a crucial part of the interview process, because the last few lines you say to the interviewer might be the ones that are remembered the most. In a way, wrapping up an interview can be considered like the closing of a sale. In addition to thanking the interviewer for taking the time to interview you, your words should be full of power and should reinforce the idea that you are looking forward to working for the company. You could say something along the lines of the following:

- Thank you very much for your time. I look forward to working with you.
- I look forward to continuing our conversation.
- I enjoyed our conversation, and I would be glad to work for you. This sounds like an ideal position for me.

At the same time, try not to sound overconfident. Avoid expressions such as "I look forward to hearing from you soon" and "I am excited to be a part of this company (this project)."

The next step after the interview is to follow up—the same day—with a brief, polite e-mail, thanking the interviewer for consideration and reiterating your desire for the job.

Summary

1. Research has shown that for many jobs, the first twenty to thirty seconds of an interview play a critical role toward receiving a final offer.
2. The candidate must start by arriving on time, but not too early, and introducing himself or herself with a firm handshake. Very

often the hiring manager will make the first judgement call within the first thirty seconds. Visual presentation contributes to creating a positive first impression. Being friendly, professional, honest, open, and relaxed will certainly create a great first impression.

3. Make sure you know the company. You need to have researched it and found a link between your experience and the company or position. Be precise about what you want and your experiences.

4. A hiring manager is put off by the incompatibility of ambitions to skills and expertise, which shows when a candidate cannot answer certain questions.

5. Face to face is all about making eye contact, constructing sentences well, listening well to the questions, being articulate and answering questions well, and doing a nice presentation if needed. It is difficult to pull back a bad first impression.

6. Dress code is also important. Do not give the interviewer reasons to get distracted.

7. Do you know your experience and can you describe it? "A great put-off is memorizing the entire CV. This is certainly a very big no-no! (Faiz Nazerali, Intellitech I.T. Solutions Ltd.). Most important, you need to know why you are there and who you are applying to work for. You need to research the company and prepare well for the interview.

8. Another important factor in recruiting is remuneration. When talking to recruiters it is fine to talk about it, because they will try to place you in your salary range. But when talking to the hiring manager, never speak about it unless you are asked a direct question.

9. Compare the end of an interview with closing a sale. End with a strong salutation or statement, and follow up—same day—with a brief, polite e-mail, thanking the interviewer for consideration and reiterating your desire for the job.

CHAPTER 6

Graduate positions—having the right mix

You are studying hard (I hope!) during your undergraduate or postgraduate degree, or maybe you are about to graduate from university in the next few months. But once you have finished your studies, the most important and difficult part begins: you need to find a job! How do you do it? How do you even start?

> *One thing is needed by people who have no experience: Attitude! If you have the right attitude to succeed, then you have a good chance of being successful.*
>
> *Daniel Singham, Toluna*

At least once in your life you have walked into a coffee shop and been served by someone who has a master's degree. You have certainly spoken at some point with one of your former classmates who shared with you his or her frustration at being unemployed despite having completed a degree course, maybe even with top marks. University fees are increasing. On the other hand, there seems to be no correlation between higher fees and better opportunities for landing a dream job or even just a good job in the student's industry of choice. What is missing, and why do some graduates fail to find a job immediately after university?

Businesses always welcome humble people who have the drive to succeed and are always ready to give more than what is demanded by them in their contract.

Luca Benigni, Benigni&K

What are the key characteristics an employer is looking for when hiring junior candidates or graduates with little to no experience? From the responses I received in the interviews for this book, I believe that the right candidate usually has the right mix of the following:

- Reputation of the university attended
- Grades achieved in coursework
- Work experience during school
- Additional skills
- Successful interview

Reputation of the university attended

This is the most controversial area of discussion. In many countries, graduating from a top university has always been strongly correlated with success in the labor market. The highest caliber universities, often private and extremely expensive, used to guarantee a top job in the student's area of interest. Furthermore, a high grade point average was always a good entry point for a graduate applying for postgraduate positions. Is that still the case?

I am fascinated by the variety of answers I have received from the respondents to my research. According to many, graduating from a top university is still considered a key way to distinguish yourself, especially for certain professions. One of the respondents who requested to be anonymous confirmed that "a large majority of companies would reserve a certain percentage of positions for those candidates coming from bulge-bracket universities to preserve the reputation of the company." Many consider the education provided by top universities as strict and of high quality; students graduating from top universities are believed to have studied harder than other students, so they are highly regarded by potential employers. Others believe that because people who study at top universities pay a much higher fee to attend their path toward graduation will be easier; it would be in the university's interest to have a high number of successful graduates finishing their studies faster than the average and achieving outstanding grades.

Access to alumni networks

In the opinion of many of the experts consulted for this book, people attend top universities (or postgraduate business schools) because they provide them the opportunity to connect with a strong network. Remember the speed networking we talked about in chapter 4? Regardless of whether top universities prepare their students better or worse for the labor market than do other universities, top universities offer the opportunity to be part of a stronger alumni network that will help in the job search directly or indirectly. You will not only study with a group of students who might be well connected and possibly relatives of individuals who have high net worth but you will also have plenty of managers and recruiters from top firms coming to campus to give seminars and advertise their own firms. A year ago I was in the process of trying to change jobs, repositioning myself for a different role within a similar industry. While I was trying to network with like-minded individuals, someone wrote the following to me:

> Working in finance doesn't matter; speaking three languages doesn't matter; having an MBA most definitely counts for nothing; managing people counts for nothing; the subject you study doesn't really matter. If you want to get into a firm, the only way to stack the odds in your favor is the school you go to and the network that you create for yourself. Being interesting and easy to get along with will help a lot as well. If you go to a good university, you will have more career events in a week than you can physically attend. These events will be attended by the people in charge of hiring, both actual

team managers and HR professionals within the field you are interested in. Not being an idiot and being easy to get along with are how people end up getting these jobs.

Although attending a highly ranked university will facilitate the job search and many people still think this way, there are plenty of graduates from top universities who struggle to find work! On the other hand, I also am aware of plenty of people in my network who, despite having studied at less well-known universities, have progressed significantly in their careers and achieved a lot at young ages. **If you are not attending or have not attended a top university, there is always a way!** I think the key concept here is awareness. You should not wait until the last year of university to start thinking about your future career. Job search starts in year one of university. Look for people in your sector of interest. Try to connect with them. Ask them what their day is like and what their job is like. Gain an understanding of what it takes to succeed in their jobs and how you can acquire the relevant skills to work at their firms. Try to get a summer internship at their firms. Build additional skills outside the academic world, because companies need people able to act in the real world in real situations and with real skills. Cristiano Cardarelli, Contract Excellence Manager, believes that "if the person does not have access to the best universities and networks, he or she will need to work and study hard and find other ways to shine, including achieving higher than average grades, gaining extra skills, and accumulating work experience prior to graduation."

In the next few paragraphs we will discuss alternative ways for people who have not attended a top university to be successful. Remember, there is always a way!

Grades achieved in coursework

Graduating with high grades is important but not as important as attending a good university. Nowadays a large majority of young people go to university after high school. Twenty-five to thirty years ago graduates still comprised a minority of the population, but today in most developed countries a large percentage of people go to university. This means that when an employer is looking to hire young graduates, he or she will necessarily focus on certain criteria to skim through the CVs and pick the best ones. What is important is having the right combination of university, reputation, and grades. Graduating relatively fast is also noteworthy: "It means being straight to the point and able to avoid wasting time. It means good time-management and organizational skills. Graduating with strong grades means perfectionism. Doing both together is excellence. And if the degree is from a good university it means also having good knowledge of your sector or area of expertise or studies." (Mishelle Sassun, Bee Creations). Consistent with the phenomenon of globalization, people often live in two or three countries during their studies and the first years of their careers. In addition, thousands of institutions offer graduate degrees. The manager, HR director, or headhunter working on a round of recruiting will usually receive plenty of CVs for the open positions. In many cases, unless the candidate studies at a top university, the manager will not be able to evaluate him or her from only the grade point average and the name of the university—most likely the manager will not know the differences among universities, courses studied, and their levels of difficulty. Grades are relevant only in relation to the rank of the university.

I managed teams speaking seven different languages and coming from ten different countries. When hiring someone who comes from a different country, it is really difficult to understand the nuances of their university degrees— how difficult or easy it is to get good grades, how long it typically takes to earn a degree, and what style of studies is predominant in the candidate's country of origin.
Mishelle Sassun, Bee Creations

Grades achieved are certainly important; however, I would tend to stress the university attended over grades, as it is easier to achieve high grades if you are graded on a curve and your competition is not as good.
Michael O'Brien, BNY Mellon

In some cases the internal recruiter, HR, and even the portal on which you upload your CV will discount any applicant whose grade point average is below a specified level as part of a prescreening process.

The manager doesn't even see your application unless you approach him or her directly, a case is made for you based on a recommendation, or you are an experienced hire with a skill set that is difficult to find. The importance of your grade point average? If you went to a top university in the UK, for example, and you earned a degree such as math or engineering, a 2:2 is unlikely to hold you back. If you are an experienced hire with a recommendation or a desired skill set, a 2:1 would be great but not the only deciding factor for most companies.

Victoria Barry-Woods, Allegis Group

More than in the past, managers are actually open to any type of candidate and might even view candidates from top universities or with top marks with suspicion because of reputation.

As practice shows, none of the two (grades and university brand) are of crucial importance. It is often the case that people from good universities who have good grades are incapable of dealing with others, resolving issues, and so on.

Julia Faida, Optimum Media

It is, however, very important to try to graduate from university with at least a certain minimum grade point average. A young university student must understand from the beginning of his or her university career the minimum grade accepted within his or her desired market, industry, or graduate programs. "Most companies will ask candidates to have higher grades in order to apply. It will be prequalifying criteria. If you do not have a sufficient grade, then the university you attended becomes irrelevant," states Daniel Singham of Toluna. As an Italian having studied in Italy and the United Kingdom, I was well aware that I needed to achieve at least a 100 out of 110 grade from an Italian university if I wanted to have a career in Italy. When

I moved abroad and settled in the United Kingdom, I was also well aware that graduating with at least a 2:1 final mark was paramount. A university student must ensure that he or she studies hard enough to reach at least that grade point average. Focusing on getting good grades is not enough, however. If you were to ask me *"Should I study harder to get top grades or should I find an internship and do some networking?"* my answer would certainly be internship and networking! When you are at university, you should do your best to get top grades, but on the other hand you need to think about your exit strategy, like for any investment. What is the return on the investment made by you or your parents for you to attend university? The best return on the investment is finding a job, hopefully a job you enjoy, rather quickly after graduation. Top grades will not necessarily get you a job. But a good contact, maybe established while doing an internship, can take you far. Although studying hard and earning good grades are important, other factors that will affect the job search for young graduates are networking and work experience. Young university students should be aware of their own markets and look at the job markets before graduating. Seek a recruiter's advice at the very beginning of your studies. Gain a clear understanding of what you want to do in the future. After talking to a recruiter, you might even be able to choose optional courses that your future employers might like. Recruiters and experienced professionals could help you get a summer internship during your second year at university and provide you with further guidance and opportunities for your future.

Work experience during school

Young graduates, I recommend starting everywhere. Do it very well, get your hands dirty, and you will progress within that industry.

Pritul Khagram, People Force International

"For a graduate with no experience on the CV, it is extremely difficult to find a job. Over ten years ago, a person would start working after university with no experience. Nowadays you need to have done something meaningful—especially if entering in finance, law, consultancy, or higher degrees—at least during one of the summers during your university years. Or you do an apprenticeship, one year of experience during your studies or one of those courses where you work while you study. You need to have something, and it has to be meaningful rather than working at the corner store. Work experience is infinitely more important." (Julia Barber, Cornell Partnership). This statement describes one of the most important aspects of graduates' recruiting today. Students need to learn how to work from a very young age, testing the work environment during the summer, and building their CVs. "My clients all perceive well recent graduates who have shown from a young age that they have the drive and ambition to succeed in the future. They have, for example, found a job during the three months of summer holidays while in high school or university," states an anonymous financial recruiter based in London.

Until just a few years ago, it was rare for university students to work throughout university. In the majority of cases, candidates would earn their university degrees and start sending their CV to firms with nothing listed under work experience. The only factor distinguishing candidates was the grade point average. A manager recruiting for entry-level and junior positions could receive a bunch of CVs from recent graduates who had all completed the same degree and probably with the majority of them having achieved a similar grade point average. This is no longer the case. With more and more young people graduating from top universities, many companies are demanding work experience from job applicants. Most of the interviewers I spoke to recognize the value of those who really pushed to gain relevant work experience.

In the last ten years, the mismatch between university programs and the job market has deepened. There are important differences between knowledge (what you study), skills (what you can do), and abilities (competence in an activity or occupation because of your skill, training, or other qualification). The mismatch forces a growing number of recent graduates to accept jobs they feel they are academically overqualified for or to study more. But the graduate is suffering from a misconception. He or she has the knowledge but needs to learn how to apply it and use it, how to accumulate actual skills and abilities. That is why you need to accept the entry-level job, accumulate skills, and then move on.

Differences among skills, knowledge, and abilities

Knowledge is theoretical or practical understanding of a subject. For example, an employee might have knowledge of SWOT (strengths, weaknesses, opportunities, and threats) analysis used in evaluating business opportunities. That doesn't mean the employee is a business analyst able to analyze large projects or has the skills to be a CEO capable of selling a business to one or more investors.

Skills, on the other hand, are the proficiencies developed through training or experience. Using the SWOT analysis example, the employee needs to demonstrate skills in performing a SWOT analysis of a real business or product. Skills are usually learned by doing. We can develop skills by the application of knowledge to practical work experience.

Abilities are the qualities of being able to do something. There is a fine line between skills and abilities. Most people would say the difference is whether the item in question was learned (skill) or innate (ability). I think of the capacity for analysis and logical thought as abilities that can help an employee develop SWOT analysis skills. Competence in an activity or occupation can also refer to specific talents, special skills, or aptitudes.

Having the right mix

A hiring manager or recruiter would expect to see from a recent graduate a mix of work and life experiences that show he or she can cope with the changing dynamics of today's work environment.

Having worked during university, you will show the manager you are capable of working hard and multitasking (working and studying).

For a graduate with no experience on the CV, it is extremely difficult to find a job. Over ten years ago, a person would start working after university with no experience. Nowadays you need to have done something meaningful—especially if entering in finance, law, consultancy, or higher degrees— at least during one of the summers during your university years. Or you do an apprenticeship, one year of experience during your studies or one of those courses where you work while you study. You need to have something, and it has to be meaningful rather than working at the corner store. Work experience is infinitely more important. A lot of interviewers and HR professionals recognize the value of those who really pushed themselves to get extra work experience. Many universities do not have a career program, but there is a way to get around that. You need more personality and to push harder, because most people have a degree nowadays.

Julia Barber, Cornell Partnership

As Julia Barber describes it, work experience is not meant to be "working at the corner store." The work must be something "meaningful." But what is meaningful? Meaningful work is relevant to your studies and career goals. Many companies currently offer summer internship programs. Such programs are often combinations of very basic tasks assigned to interns during busy periods and relevant training that will help the interns put their academic knowledge into practice. Economics and business student should therefore seek internships at banks or financial institutions, marketing students should look for marketing experience, aspiring journalists should seek experience at a newspaper or digital agency, law students should find internships at law firms, and engineering students should find relevant work experience at firms that employ engineers.

The experience is not only useful in building the CV. Such internships also provide you with references that a potential employer can check before making you an offer. References can stay in your CV for years if you maintain the relationships, and they will help you with not only your first job but also many more opportunities in the future. Internships are also a great way to start networking. During an internship you will work every day with managers who may be able to connect you to other managers in your sector of interest or expertise. Most important, they might make you an offer in the near future. These internships can be stepping stones for internal recruiting and for future networking. It is not uncommon to hear about a candidate who started working at a firm as an intern, showed great talent, and was made permanent staff. In fact, most banks hire summer interns, evaluate them at the end of the summer, and then make full-time offers.

How early should students look for internships? The sooner, the better. A few years ago it was rare for graduates to have work experience, but now it is common. Who will stand out? Most likely, not just the candidates who have one work experience but the candidates who have several different work experiences before graduation. If you are a parent, start thinking about the future of your sons and daughters sooner rather than later. Financial institutions such as Nomura offer internships in various areas of finance and IT to people as young as sixteen years old, teenagers who are still in high school. These opportunities range from insight programs for high school students (sixteen to seventeen years old), preinternship programs for first- or second-year university students, internship programs for third-year university students, six- to twelve-month industrial placement programs, and full-time opportunities for recent graduates. This is a trend, and the trend will continue in the next years. Again, the sooner you start accumulating work experience, the better. "If you have worked since the age of sixteen, that shows you have a desire to make ends meet," says Michael Witte of Capgemini.

The middle experience

Because entry-level positions are not as abundant as they were in the past, an employer will start looking at the perfect match between university and position for junior positions. Although there used to be several opportunities for graduates to start a career in a business field despite having studied humanities subjects, these opportunities are becoming rare. Changing your field after graduation is now extremely difficult.

I started my university career with an undergraduate degree in international relations. My dream was to become an ambassador. I gradually realized I was more interested in economics and business while studying those subjects that were considered "minor" during my studies. After a brief program spent at the United Nations in New York City in partnership with my university, I realized I was no longer interested in becoming an ambassador but instead wanted to pursue a career in business. I found two internships in the marketing; they gave me a great foundation for many areas of business and how organizations work. At the end of the second internship, I was accepted to start an MBA in marketing and management. Eventually I ended up working in a management capacity at a market intelligence and investor relations consulting firm. I am now a different type of ambassador: I represent a company rather than a country. What a journey, you might think: from dreaming of becoming an ambassador, to studying marketing, to becoming a manager in the investor relations sector! It was not the most straightforward journey of education and career development. Would it be possible to make such a change from one course to another, from one career to another, in the current labor market? I believe it would be very difficult but not impossible. In my case, the "middle experience" in marketing helped me to gain an MBA in marketing and management and eventually end up working in a management capacity and apply the management skills learned from the MBA program. The "middle experience" concept introduced by Julia Barber (Cornell Partnership) worked extremely well in my case. While you study or while you work, it is important to have something that will connect you to a specific job or career, something that is not necessarily the major of your educational degree or the key area of specialty in your work.

A person I know moved from being a telecom equity analyst to being a generalist analyst with focus on both telecom and oil and gas. After some time, he became an oil and gas analyst only. This means that the middle experience was very important. He would have not been able to move easily from telecom to oil and gas without the middle experience.
Julia Barber, Cornell Partnership

I am not sure where I would be today if my parents had not been able to afford to pay for my MBA, but the MBA was extremely important for me to change course from international relations and my teenaged dream of becoming an ambassador to instead end up working in management. If you are reading this book thinking about your career and you are not sure exactly what you want to be, stop now and take a deep breath. Put your studies aside for a few days, and read and research about different careers. Think about what you want to be in your life. Is there something you may have never thought about doing but now seems interesting to you? Do some research on the topic. The Internet will do, but even better, can you find someone to talk to about the field? Look at Internet blogs and LinkedIn, talk to people you know, talk to a recruiter. Ask the questions that will help you understand what that job or career you want is really all about. After you have researched, does it still interest you? If so, find something that can lead you there. Can you change elective courses in your university program and add some subjects more relevant to your new interest? Or will you get a master's degree? Are you still confused? Talk to your academic advisor or speak to a mentor who can direct you and enlighten you.

If you are a young person coming out of university from a course and then you realize you want to do something completely different, go back to school. You cannot think

about what you want to do in your life when you have finished university. You need to think about it while at university.
Cristiano Cardarelli, Contract Excellence Manager

Additional skills

Earning a degree is a very important and difficult part of a person's life, but degree programs are often disconnected from the real world. Bachelor's degrees usually provide a general and broad knowledge of a subject, but the graduate will most likely be unable to apply any of the concepts studied to the real world. Once hired into a real job, the graduate will be trained by the company. In an incredibly large proportion of cases, he or she will never apply any of the knowledge learned at university. Because a recent graduate will probably be trained in the new job, what are the most important additional skills an employer looks for? By far, they are languages and IT skills. In some professions, only one of the two will be relevant, but in others a combination of the two is always highly regarded. Such languages are those currently considered most relevant in the business world, such as German, Spanish, French, Russian, Portuguese, Chinese, Japanese, and Arabic. Relevant IT skills begin with the most basic ability to use a computer and Microsoft Office, with Excel being the most important program of the Microsoft Office Package, and Microsoft PowerPoint (a program used in creating presentations) the second most important. There is also a broad range of advanced IT skills; different fields have their own popular programs, and it is important for students or new graduates to be aware of them. In finance, for example, advanced IT skills highly regarded by employers include programming languages such as VBA, C#, C++, and Java. If you are an architect, an employer will expect you to be able to use the program CAD.

A successful interview

All right, you did a great job in getting the right combination of university reputation, grades achieved, work experience while studying, and additional skills. A potential employer has called you in for an interview. One thing is missing, though, and it is the only one that will matter in the end. You must have to have a successful interview. What is HR or the hiring manager looking for? "People who are confident and have good communication skills—possible leaders of the future. Fragile, shy people are obviously not good, because the employer cannot put them in front of clients," says Pritul Khagram of People Force International Ltd. Mishelle Sassun of Bee Creations looks at what she describes as "determination, the sparkle of those who want to succeed no matter how much effort it will cost them. If this exists, it means they are ready to overcome difficulties and learn all they can." She continues, "Secondly, I normally look for character traits that match the job and role they need to cover. You cannot hire a shy person for a sales job or an impatient person for an analyst job. If the traits do not match, they will not enjoy the job in the first place, it will be very difficult to motivate them, and overall, they will hardly excel in the job."

According to Delphine Lecluze of Orient Capital, "traditional interviews tend to focus on competencies, and candidates can provide well-rehearsed answers. However, more and more interviews are now strength- and personality-based interviews, which help establish if the candidate will be a good and long-term fit, if he or she will naturally love the job and strive in it. It is difficult to prepare for these types of interviews, as candidates can't search for the answers on Google. Strength-based interviewing helps the employer get to know the real person behind the candidate. When I interview candidates, I pay attention to the body language, the posture, the speech patterns, the facial expressions, and the nerves. These factors help me to decide if the candidate is right for the role and to detect lies." Let's analyze these two types of interviews in more detail in the following paragraphs.

Competency-based interviews

The terms competence and competency can be confused. In truth the two terms mean the same thing, in that they are both used as a word that means a required behavior within a job role. However, competence is more often used when describing a basic minimum level of job performance and competency would be more commonly understood as a description of performance excellence. Competency-focused questions are commonly used in interviews today and stump people the most. The hiring manager will usually focus on a combination of technical questions and behavioral questions. Examples of behavioral questions are "Tell me how you would react in this scenario," and "Think about a situation XYZ and solve the issue based on what you learned in your university studies." More than behavior, these questions gauge the individual's approach and reactions to various situations. Many employers will expect you to use the Situation, Task, Action, and Result (STAR) technique to answer such questions. The STAR format is a behavioral job interview technique interviewers use to gather all relevant information about a specific capability required for the job.

- Situation—The interviewer wants you to present a recent challenging situation you experienced.
- Task—What did you have to achieve in the situation? The interviewer wants to understand your goal in the situation.
- Action—What did you do? The interviewer wants information about what you did, why you did it, and what the potential alternatives were.
- Results—What was the outcome of your actions? What did you achieve, and did you meet your objectives? What did you

learn from the experience, and have you applied the learning since then?

"Tell me how you decided on your university." "How did you move on to your next role at company XYZ?" "Why do you want to work for us?" "What are your reasons for wanting to switch jobs?" Competency-based questions can become incredibly specific when the recruiter or hiring manager asks specifically how you could apply certain skills or competencies learned in a previous job or at university to the new position. Such questions can also be tricky, because the manager might not know what to expect as an answer, and therefore the candidate must answer very clearly and in a detailed manner. Explain how the organization will benefit from hiring you, perhaps even putting the benefit in financial terms.

In my role as a recruiter, the qualifications play a small part. The strength in the candidate's responses acts as the main decider of whether I am to offer the role of underwriter to the individual.

Tosin Ojikutu, Investec

Bottom line, if you are going to an interview and you know you have a specific relevant skill set, be prepared to demonstrate how to apply those skills. Failure to demonstrate practical knowledge and apply it to a specific job will automatically disqualify you for a position.

Personality-focused interviews

I am very surprised about the attitudes of people, especially young ones, who despite the current financial environment want a lot here and now but do not want to commit and invest their time and energy into work. Our company hires people who have no experience for junior positions so that we can train them from scratch. The most important thing for

an entry-level position is the individual's personal skills, such as motivation, ability to assume responsibility, and desire to learn. They need to be prepared to work extra.
Julia Faida, Optimum Media

The candidate must have the right attitude, the right personality. In many cases, managers are not necessary looking for specific skills or the perfect match. The 100 percent candidate, who has all skills and requirements for the specific job, is usually sitting on a high salary and will command a premium to change jobs. On the other hand, managers often look for the imperfect match that could become the perfect one. Most important, they look for a good fit with the existing team. Hardworking is certainly an attribute required by all jobs, but hard work no longer means working longer hours than your contract. The nine-to-five job is only a dream for many today. With smartphones, your manager and clients can reach you at almost any time of day and any day of the week.

Compare yourself to a machine...(almost) ALWAYS available whether at work or outside working hours, WILLING to work hard and go the extra mile, to be flexible.
Faiz Nazerali, Intellitech I.T. Solutions Ltd.

In a market with fewer opportunities and jobs, it is easy to find situations in which the few people employed at a firm must work harder than would have been expected a few years ago. As a manager, I have interviewed hundreds of candidates, and I never heard anyone tell me "I am ready to work hard and any extra hours or weekends needed." This is what I am looking for. Had I heard this sentence, most likely I would have offered the candidate the job. And this is what many managers out there are looking for. But besides being able to work hard beyond your regular contractual hours, you need to show you are an efficient, effective worker who gets results. If you just sit there and work hard but do not achieve results, there is no point in working hard.

Many candidates attend the interview thinking they are the best possible hires for the company. They think about what they can offer and are sure it is what the manager wants. And they think that they have what nobody else does. Wrong! Most graduates are exactly the same. They have attended an educational program where other hundreds of candidates have studied, and even more students will have studied a similar course at other universities in the same country. Comparing several people with the same exact education, who would you choose? You would most likely choose the person who can show you that he or she will work as hard as necessary. Harder than anyone else the manager is interviewing.

Hard work is more important than the actual degree. I like to see the candidate's muscles.

Sheryl Cusia, Boudicca Proxy

Summary

1. The reputation of the university attended is still considered a key way to distinguish candidates, especially for certain professions. Some companies reserve a certain percentage of positions for candidates from bulge-bracket universities to preserve the company's reputation.
2. Attending a good university also provides access to a better alumni network. Graduating with a high grade point average is important but not as important as attending a good university.
3. There are, however, plenty of ways someone who has not attended a top university can become successful. The key concept here is awareness, because one should not wait until the last year of university to start thinking about a future career. The job search and CV building starts in year one of university.
4. To succeed in today's job market, new graduates must have the right combination of attributes: a) reputation of the university attended, b) grades achieved in coursework, c)

work experience during school, d) additional skills, and e) a successful interview. Having the right attitude and being humble are also characteristics needed by young people to succeed in today's job market.

5. Candidates now need to have some sort of work experience on their CVs before applying for jobs. They need to have done something meaningful and relevant before completing their studies, especially if they are entering fields such as finance, law, or consulting or applying to graduate degree programs. Universities give a student knowledge, but the student must turn that knowledge into skills and abilities.

6. Employers look for candidates who have specific additional skills that are rare in the market. The most important additional skills employers look for are languages and IT skills.

7. There are two types of interviews. Traditional interviews tend to focus on competencies, and candidates can provide well-rehearsed answers. Competency-based interviews, in contrast, are commonly conducted today; they focus on a combination of technical and behavioral questions. Many employers will expect candidates to use the Situation, Actual, Task, and Result (STAR) technique to answer such interview questions.

CHAPTER 7

Moving across industries and functions—career changers

S ome sectors of the job market are currently stagnant. Some have been for many years. A number of professions are disappearing or evolving, while public-sector recruitment is down in many areas, and some organizations are freezing hiring. Companies have had to cut budgets and benefits due to the recession and are no longer the dream workplaces they used to be. The resignation rate is lower than the layoff rate. People just do not want to take a risk, hence the labor market is stagnant. If you are currently frustrated by the lack of jobs in your particular field or career opportunities at your company, why not explore new horizons? Should people who have worked in sectors hit hard by the current economic situation change careers to improve their chances of finding jobs? Yes, provided they are prepared that the challenges associated with changing direction: it can take months or even years, often involves some sort of retraining and pay cut, and there is a risk to that the person will end up in sector that is also stagnant or lacks jobs.

Who is this career changer? In a nutshell, a career changer is a person who is trying to change roles. There are three main categories of career changers:

a) *A person who switches from one industry to another but applies skills from the previous job to the new job. Examples are an HR manager or accountant who moves from a company in one industry to one in a different industry.*

b) *A person who stays in the same industry but changes to a job that relies on different skills than did the previous job. Examples are a banker who switches from being an investment banker to being a private banker and a person who remains in the same industry but moves from operations to sales.*

c) *A person who makes a complete change, a combination of job change and industry change.*

Some companies actually promote the idea of hiring career changers: "We are open to career changers, because lots of people are laid off because of the crisis not because they are not good. If a person has achieved goals and targets, we are happy to consider him," states Antonio Iandolo of DB Apparel. Michael Witte of Capgemini states that his company considers career changers and actually promotes the idea too. "I personally think it is not a bad idea to have, for example, folks with a finance background going into service delivery and client-facing roles. I would personally consider a career-changer candidate with strong, transferable skills, depending on personality, desire to succeed, and the specific role I was hiring for," he continues. Some industries facilitate opportunities for career changers, because they are niche industries and suffer from a scarcity of candidates who have the right skills. "Managers often hire career changers, because finding people with the requisite experience is not easy," says Michael O'Brien of BNY Mellon. You should consider whether there a scarcity of candidates with the right skills in your area. If there is, you might be able to enter your new area of interest easily or with relatively less effort than in other industries. If, however, "you are trying to enter a growing industry that requires specific skills, you need to be pretty spectacular to be hired and know somebody that will help you get your foot into the industry," states Kelly Blokdijk of Talent Talks.

Experience is key. Career changers must find a way to acquire that experience and skills. The two most common options are to engage in further education or to get an entry-level job in the chosen industry.

Graduate studies vs. work experience

Cristiano Cardarelli, Julia Barber, Faiz Nazerali, and Julia Faida have all outlined the importance of qualifications. They indicate that the person must be serious about the career change and not just "testing the waters." According to Tosin Ojikutu (Investec), Cindy Anastasi (CCBill EU), and Michael O'Brien (BNY Mellon), it is possible to acquire and practice new skills in one's free time; however, graduate degrees our qualifications are more quantifiable from a potential employer's perspective.

> *What is the best way for career changers to approach a different industry? New skills acquired by reading or practicing in one's free time are important, because they demonstrate a genuine interest, which is important in having confidence that the applicant is the right fit and will stay for the long term. So I consider them greatly. But graduate degrees and qualifications are more quantifiable, and thus, easier to compare.*
> *Michael O'Brien, BNY Mellon*

> *We accept people who study on their own time if they can prove what they know and they are able to apply basic concepts.*
> *Cindy Anastasi, CCBill EU*

> *I am interested in candidates who have gained new qualifications as well as those who have learned new skills just by reading or practicing in one's own free time, because this shows initiative.*
> *Tosin Ojikutu, Investec*

The majority of experts, however, are very skeptical about career changers and how a graduate qualification can help. Companies really want candidates with knowledge of the niche; a complete career change is extremely difficult, but changing jobs within a sector is slightly easier.

> *A master's degree is not very relevant for a career changer. I look at the experience. Do you have it? If not, I am not going to waste my time. Having a master's does not necessarily mean you can do the job. It is definitely an outstanding achievement, and it tells me you can possibly do the job. But do you have any experience? It is risky for people who study too much, because the recruiter or the manager could think the person will get bored in a few weeks. I would not send a career changer to any of my clients if the person has no experience. If the person is looking for an entry-level position, maybe I could consider hiring him or her. But slightly higher roles are difficult. Clients provide strict guidelines, and the recruiter has to follow them. The only exception is when the person knows the recruiter well and the recruiter knows the hiring manager well. It comes down to contacts.*
>
> *Anonymous financial industry recruiter,*
> *London, United Kingdom*

Here we go back to the concept of knowledge vs. skills. Indeed, a master's degree can help, but we must emphasize the importance of on-the-job learning, which provides professionals with the skills needed to actually perform in a job. Bottom line, a recruiter places candidates for their skills rather than their knowledge. "Graduate degrees very often are just another line on a CV; very often the master's, which should be investment in a person's career, is actually an investment in one's debt," states Pritul Khagram of People Force International. "New qualifications may help, but I am more interested in experience and attitude." (Daniel Singham, Toluna) Julia Barber of Cornell Partnership states: "unless the master's is incredibly specific, get an entry-level job rather than a master's." "Nobody even looks at graduate degrees. Nobody ever looked at me for my two master's, and I have never hired anyone based on their master's. There is no direct connection, in my opinion, between having a master's and being successful looking for a job," states Angelo Chirulli of LEXeFISCAL. He argues that working hard on the CV can be better than engaging in further education: "I am open to career changers, because we all know the market we are working in at the moment— it's tough. In the past people used to do a master's to reposition their profiles. Now I would just customize the CV very well and work hard on highlighting similarities across sectors; again, I don't think a master's alone will help." Transferable skills. Once again, based on the feedback received from Angelo Chirulli, it comes down to the importance of transferable skills in today's market.

With similar arguments, Kelly Blokdijk of Talent Talks discourages people from engaging in further education without having any experience in the chosen industry: "It is mistakenly understood that more degrees make people more marketable; in reality, the majority of entry-level jobs do not require an advanced degree. Even when a degree is listed as a required qualification, employers tend to prioritize experience over education. The most marketable job candidates display a balanced combination of formal education and work experience in the field." It is clear from most of the interviews I conducted for this book that graduate degrees should combine specialized education with additional experience within the field of interest, whether via internships, freelance projects, or another avenue.

There seems to be a common line of thought among the experts, especially with regard to the idea of quitting a job to obtain a master's degree; it is expressed very well by Cindy Anastasi and Paolo Garonna:

I would never encourage people to quit their jobs and go to studies.

Cindy Anastasi, CCBill EU

I would much rather have an income and study than just study, get a master's, and not be employable. There is no employer out there ready to hire you because you have a master's or a PhD. One thing is sure: career changers have to invest time, effort, and energy in changing career. They need to obtain new skills and become part of a new "family."

Paolo Garonna, Federazione Banche Italiane

Changing career: where to start

Let's face it. If you are planning to change career, your job does not fulfill you, your sector is not doing well, or worse, you hate your job. These are all fine reasons to justify a career change. But where do you start? You are changing career, so you probably think you need to start by accepting the fact that you will take a pay cut, give up your seniority, or just start from a lower position in the new organization you have in your current organization. But why not instead shoot for a job that is a step up from the one you currently have? How can you do that if you are moving out of your sector of expertise? But do you really need to change sector to change career?

Remember, a career change can also be a change in role within the same industry. Consider the following scenario: You list the things you love to do and, in a separate list, the things you are good at. You will see overlaps between the two lists but also realize you are very good at things you no longer want to do. The mismatches are the main reasons you want to change career. Take the time to reflect once again whether the change is feasible and worth it—economically and personally. In the list of things you are good at you might find a unique skill that is very rare in the market. Employers pay a premium for people who have that rare skill. You hate doing it on a daily basis, and that is the main reason you want to change career. But have you ever thought of becoming a manager in charge of a team that you can train to do exactly what you hate doing? Because you are amazing at doing that job, you may also be amazing at teaching it to other people. They will eventually do the job; you will only mentor them and supervise their work.

OK, we understood that even though you could progress within your sector to a more senior position by leveraging the skills you don't like, you see a complete career change as the only feasible option. I read an interesting article online that said any individual should focus on moving to a job that will put the individual closer to his or her personal goals. The only way to get better at something is to do more of it. Can you do more of the work you love in your next job? LinkedIn is a fantastic resource for people thinking about making a job or career change. How many millions of profiles and job openings do you see on LinkedIn? By taking your time to browse LinkedIn, you'll get ideas for your own career. Use the Advanced People Search page (look for the word Advanced next to the open search bar at the top of most LinkedIn pages) to browse the LinkedIn's vast database of users by searching for key words. Choose key words that interest you, like "responsible investment," "real estate," "investor relations," "commercial law," or whatever you're passionate about. You should also include in the search the city where you would ideally like to live. If you are in London and want to stay in London, specify London. If you want to relocate to the United States, specify New York or a different city there. You will not only get ideas for your career direction but you will also identify specific employers that you may not have been aware of until now, in your desired area.

Your next question might be, "Paolo, even if I choose a career direction that interests me, how do I go back and change my work experience in my CV to make it look relevant to the field I'm interested in now?" That's an easy question to answer. Write your CV focusing on your strengths and unique selling points (it's better if these are transferrable skills), and highlight them as much as you can in your CV. Then what? Which job search channels are available to a career changer? Headhunters are a great channel, if you have a recruiter-friendly résumé. That means that your résumé and experiences make you look like you were raised in a petri dish to do a job that employers need done. It is easy to find out whether your résumé is recruiter-friendly. Find a recruiter in your area on LinkedIn, and call the recruiting firm's office directly. Ask to speak with the recruiter you have identified and, once connected, ask him or her, "I found you on LinkedIn, and I wondered whether you might have a moment to glance at my CV." The recruiter will probably ask you a few questions about your background and figure out quickly whether you're a recruiter-friendly candidate at this point in your career. If not, no worries. You can use the best job-search channel of all, direct outreach to hiring managers. You can find hiring managers using the same Advanced People Search on LinkedIn that we have already described or other channels such as networking, casual meetings at conferences or business clubs, inviting people out for coffee. Most important, you do not need to see a job ad posted. The hiring might not have an opening right now but will remember you when there is one.

Linking personal interests to transferable skills

Performing a thorough personal audit is a good start to the process of initiating a career change. What are your goals, interests, strengths, and key skills? There is one critical aspect to most people's career change. The key concept is transferable skills.

> *We do not consider career changers, but we could possibly consider one with strong transferable skills and proven achievement in a different field. However, career changers indicate a personal issue with being indecisive. New qualifications help the career changer, because they indicate that the applicant is serious about the change of career and not just "testing the waters."*
> *Faiz Nazerali, Intellitech I.T. Solutions Ltd.*

Everyone has transferable skills (most likely based on personality type), but most people acquire additional transferable skills during any job, regardless of the career the person has undertaken. Transferable skills can be a major asset for a career changer. These skills can be applied to an entirely new field that may have many more job opportunities.

> *To date I have not successfully placed somebody from a completely different industry into another. When I have recruited for a role, within the specification the hiring manager is always looking for a similar industry or similar experience.*
> *Amina Malik, Human Resource Manager, London*

A complete career change is difficult, as confirmed by several of the respondents. Doing something in the middle—the "middle experience"—between the previous job and the career change is described by Julia Barber:

> *A person I know moved from being a telecom equity analyst to being a generalist analyst with focus on both telecom and oil and gas. After some time, he became an oil and gas analyst only. This means that the middle experience was very important. He would have not been able to move easily from telecom to oil and gas without the middle experience. A master's can be useful to vocationally ground your career. MBAs are less popular in Europe than in the United States. Some people who earn an MBA declare upfront that they are doing it for the networking opportunities. And that is where the value is. A lot of MBA graduates embark on the degree thinking they will make the so-called triple change. They expect to change function, geography, and industry. This is actually not possible. You usually can change only one of these at a time. Unless the master's is incredibly specific and you are already working in the sector, I would recommend trying to get an entry-level job within your sector of interest rather than getting a master's.*
> *Julia Barber, Cornell Partnership*

> *If you have technical knowledge, you have very limited possibilities for changing to a different sector. However, companies sometimes look for the imperfect candidate who*

could become the perfect one. You need to find a connection (something common to the two careers); otherwise, the learning curve will be too steep. The career changer must learn quickly, however. First, get a second-level education. This will provide you with a strong network, because the education (provided it is good and famous in the field) will enable you to speak to important people. These people could also look at your CV and help you refine it.

Cristiano Cardarelli, Contract Excellence Manager

We do recruit career changers, but mostly they can be accepted for entry-level or low-level positions; they need to have some relevant experience anyway. I would eventually even consider a career changer with no direct experience if he or she has a strong desire and ability to learn and might be a really valuable candidate. A good way to approach a new industry is by gaining new qualifications. I would say that degrees and courses are more reliable if one wants to evaluate the candidate quickly.

Julia Faida, Optimum Media

How easy it is to change career

Based on the responses from our interviews, not many people are keen on career changers. That is an unfortunate fact. Many people start in a sector or job specialization and then struggle to get out of it. But it depends on the circumstances of each individual and how he or she approaches the job search. Changing career is not impossible. "It depends on the reasons and how sure the candidate is about entering the new field. Companies do not like to invest time in training a person who might change his or her mind tomorrow. In such cases, a manager would normally ask many questions about the candidate's expectations and then provide a very detailed description of the job to ensure that both company and employee are sure about the expectations," states Mishelle Sassun of Bee Creations. Often HR managers are more open to career changers than are hiring managers. "HR might suggest some very good candidates, but then the hiring manager will look for very specific experience and refuse to interview a candidate. Also, managers are not interested in people whose knowledge is based on personal reading and study rather than work experience. In the current job market, I do not see many ways of changing sector without experience, to be totally honest," states Bottaro Stefano of the Opera Theatre of Rome. It is recommended that career changers who have no experience in the new area of interest avoid recruiters, regardless of newly gained qualifications. Directly approaching companies in the sector of interest provides much better chances of success. Recruiters will look for the 100 percent match between a candidate's skills and the requirements of the job advertised; they will not risk their reputation on a candidate who only might be the right fit.

The career-changer interview

Interviewers try to challenge candidates, particularly career changers, during the course of the recruitment process. The interviewer who is considering hiring a career changer must make sure the person is suitable for the job and will fit into the new company's culture and sector. The best way of dealing with the tough questions is to do your homework by researching the company. The importance of research cannot be understated; as discussed in chapter 5, you should know about the company and be prepared to answer any questions about your own CV. Of course, if there is a question for which you are not expected to know the answer or if you are genuinely stumped, don't make things up or try to bluff your way through. Move back into your comfort zone by relating the question back to something you do know and absorb any new information you are given by the interviewer. Highlight your transferrable skills and how they can be useful to your potential employer.

Conclusion

Changing careers is not easy. People attempting it need to demonstrate humility and willingness to learn. You may show the potential employer that you have skills that may be useful in the future. Most important, you need to have a certain level of humility to transition to a new career or industry. The problem for career changers is that they are often in a different league, meaning that they have different and higher-level experiences, and they sometimes struggle to adjust. I think it is important to always do something, even when you are out of a job. This is because the mind slows down and goes into a different stage when a person is not working. He or she will then need to apply a massive effort to go back to work and be productive, and employers need to keep an eye on this.

Sheryl Cusia, Boudicca Proxy

Some people complete a master's and specialize, getting education relevant to the field and contacts and experience in the industry. This is more successful, in my experience, if you complete an MBA at a top business school. A career change does not necessarily mean earning the same amount of money or moving at the same level as in the previous career. Success comes down to networking and understanding what is required to move into your chosen career. I wouldn't always advise quitting your job to change role. A person I know wanted to move from technology into procurement. She got in touch with the procurement department and worked on a project in her own time, acquiring experience without leaving her current employer. I wouldn't take the leap without relevant experience.

Victoria Barry-Woods, Allegis Group

It is hard to walk away from a stable paycheck and job security; sometimes it takes a push—like a layoff—to start you moving you in the right direction. Career change can, though, give the person a shot at a new career and a new life, later in life than for most people who are choosing a career. If you are reading this chapter and are thinking about changing your job or career, but you need to gain some relevant experience in the new area, do not simply quit your job and try to start over somewhere else. There are other options. How can you acquire experience in the field you believe will interest you? How can you build your résumé while maintaining your current position? In other words, how can you get a feeling for your newly chosen career path without taking the risk of leaving a stable job for something uncertain that you may not even like? Across the various answers received from our respondents, the following are the most common routes:

- Volunteer
- Get a part-time job in your field of interest
- Pick up a freelance job or two
- Use your vacation time to explore other industries or career fields
- Take university or vocational courses to expand your knowledge and skills
- Network with like-minded individuals employed in the field

A final recommendation comes Lisa Maghraoui of the Telecommunications Industry Association, who believes it is critically important for career changers to be 100 percent sure about quitting one job or industry for another: "Individuals who are moving from a sector that lacks jobs and opportunities should think twice before moving into a niche industry that will most likely offer the same scarcity of opportunities as the previous sector. Job seekers should also investigate the financial stability of a company before applying to it or leaving a job at a stable company for one at a company that may be less stable." I personally worked with several people who left one of my previous employers because they were frustrated with the lack of career progression; they ended up in companies with less stable financial situations that later laid them off.

Summary

1. There are three main categories of career changers: a person who switches from one industry to another but applies skills from the previous job to the new job, a person who stays in the same industry but changes to a job that relies on different skills than did the previous job, and a person who makes a complete change, a combination of job change and industry change.

2. Some industries welcome career changers because they are niche industries and suffer from a scarcity of candidates who have the right skills. However, if a candidate tries to enter a growing industry that requires specific skills, experience is key; the career changer will have to find a way to acquire that the experience and skills, whether by engaging in further education or getting an entry-level job in the chosen industry.

3. A large number of managers are, unfortunately, skeptical about career changers and how a graduate qualification can help, because companies really want candidates with knowledge of the niche. A complete career change is extremely difficult, but changing jobs within a sector is slightly easier. Experienced candidates may be able to progress within the industry, landing a more senior job at a similar or competing company.

4. Any individual should focus on moving to a job that will put the individual closer to his or her personal goals.

5. Transferable skills are the most important element used in the process of changing careers.

6. Changing careers is not easy. People attempting it need to demonstrate humility and willingness to learn. You may show the potential employer that you have skills that may come in useful in the future. Most important, you need to have a certain level of humility to transition to a new career or industry. The problem for career changers is that they are often in a different

league, with different and higher-level experiences, and they sometimes find it difficult to adjust.

7. It is important to always do something, even when out of the job market. The mind slows down and goes into a different stage when a person is not working. He or she will then need to apply a massive effort to go back to work and be productive; employers need to keep an eye on this.

8. The most common routes for beginning the process of changing career are volunteering, getting a part-time job in the new field of interest, freelancing, using vacation time to explore other industries or fields, taking university or vocational courses to expand knowledge and skills, and networking with like-minded individuals employed in the field.

CHAPTER 8

Final recommendations from the experts

A t the end of each interview conducted for this book, I asked the interviewee the following question:

With computers replacing humans and outsourcing becoming more prevalent, the job market has never been so tough. What are the two recommendations you would give job seekers for being noticed and selected by potential employers?

Below, you will find the best answers I received. In many cases, they are summarize the most important topics covered in this book.

See every interview opportunity as practice for the next role, and eventually you will find your role.

Tosin Ojikutu, Investec

I think that nowadays it is important to have more than one work experience, more than one university, and if possible, even continue to study while you are working. Add languages and maybe study in different countries. When you are young, build your CV from trainee programs, apprenticeships, and so on.

Paolo Garonna, Federazione Banche Italiane

Mobility and mentality are most important for both youngsters and older people. A fifty-year-old is as good as a twenty-five-year-old; in my opinion, age should not be in the CV. What you evaluate is the speed at which the person can learn. Most important is to adjust salary expectations. A lot of people fear managing an older employee, and this is why there is a problem. Some people never pass this stage. Put the hiring manager in a comfortable position, comfortable with hiring you. Small and medium-sized enterprises are better, because you stay and do not necessarily have expectations of progressing. The problem of many experienced hires is that they come in and think they have done it all.

Cristiano Cardarelli, Contract Excellence Manager

Learn as much as possible. Take online courses and acquire skills that you will be able to use in a job or even at home to set up a business. Acquire many practical skills via courses or volunteering. Be open to new experiences. Be different. Be adaptable. Do things in your own style. This will demonstrate you are ambitious, hardworking, and committed to work.

Sheryl Cusia, Boudicca Proxy

Do self-PR at industry events, conferences, and online communities so that you are known across the market. Never underestimate what you are doing and have done, and bear in mind the valuable experience you have acquired.

Julia Faida, Optimum Media

If you apply to an organization, check if you know anyone who works there. Finding a job is easier if you can prove to *a prospective employer that you can do the job and if there is someone credible who knows the hiring manager and can vouch for how good you are—that does more than a CV ever could. Also, the more visible you are online the better your access to opportunity and your knowledge of the market.*

Victoria Barry-Woods, Allegis Group

I would recommend to graduates to polish yourself up, practice, and put yourself in the scenario, because some companies have a ten-stage interview process. For people laid off or in their fifties and trying to change jobs, be tech-savvy and ignore your age. You need to be switched on!

Julia Barber, Cornell Partnership

Do not stick to one industry. Look at different industries. The service industry, for example, is always in need of a certain number of people.

Pritul Khagram, People Force International

Travel and learn languages. Go where work is. Detach a bit from family, because in most cases you will not find work in the city or country where you were born.

Antonio Iandolo, DB Apparel

To both young graduates and middle-aged people recently laid off, I would recommend showing passion for the role they are applying for. Young graduates should be real, honest, direct, agile, and hungry. Above all, be you, be real, be fun! Middle-aged people, on the other hand, should show some restraint. Be hungry and experienced; do not be discouraged or disenfranchised.

Michael Witte, Capgemini

Be truthful when presenting yourself. Try to be a better product than the rest, not only with better grades. Differentiate yourself with interesting experiences that enrich your profile.

Experiences in less relevant matters sometimes give your CV that little something that makes you more interesting. In general, look for a job that you are passionate about. Everyone wants someone with passion on their team.

Mishelle Sassun, Bee Creations

Use caution. Make sure that whatever role you are applying for, it is the one that will fit you for a suitable period of time.

Michael Witte, CAPGEMINI

If you are in your fifties and have been laid off, try to become a consultant, because you will get in touch with a number of people who might then lead you to getting a full-time job. If you are a new graduate, just take any job and forget about getting a job close to home.

Angelo Chirulli, LEXeFISCAL

Be very sharp with your CV and online profile. Try to be better than anyone else. For a new graduate, it is all about getting in front of people; the more people you meet the better. You need to impress them as a person. In general, the more people you know the better; on a daily basis take the opportunity to meet people nearby who might help you. Be knowledgeable about the world around you. Be educated and proactive. Become indispensable. Be better than all those people who put their heads in the sand and look unattractive.

Kelly Blokdijk, Talent Talks

If you have been laid off, before applying for a job you need to really research the company you applying to; find anything you have on the Internet, and attempt to sell yourself. You might be older and some recruiters have an issue with age, so do get the recruiting's attention and make clear why he or she should hire you; think proactively and outside the box. For young graduates, know your stuff very well and, again, research the company and be smart. Try to really get attention by knowing the fundamentals of the job that you are applying for. Never say you want to be a manager just because you have a degree. It's great to have a career path in mind, but if you're a fresh graduate with no work experience you most definitely cannot expect to take up a managerial role.

Cindy Anastasi, CCBill EU

Do not expect too much help. In the past there was a tendency to expect help from family and friends; nowadays it is a matter of personal attitude. The primary responsibility is on the individual. Engage, explore, and take risks. Do not be too picky in terms of what you like and do not like. You need to be driven by job opportunity. Do not wait to look for a job until you have to. People should always look for a job and keep an eye on the market.

Paolo Garonna, Federazione Banche Italiane

APPENDIX 1

Frequently asked interview questions

- Tell me about yourself.
- Please give me a summary of your CV.
- Please describe your role, the company, the overall culture, and the team members you work with.
- Why are you the best candidate for the job?
- Why do you want to work here?
- What is your biggest weakness?
- What is the most memorable achievement in your career?
- Why did you leave your last job? or Why do you want to leave your current job?
- What was the most challenging situation you have had at work?
- What was the best moment in your life? What was the most difficult one? How did you react to the situation and ultimately succeed?
- How did you overcome a challenging situation with a client?
- How did you manage to meet an unrealistic deadline?
- What first attracted you to your most recent role and company? What changed and when?

- You have listed xyz skill on your CV, which is very important for this role. Tell me how you have learned this skill and how you applied it in your past jobs.
- What did you like most or least about your manager?
- What did you like most and least about your team?
- What was your greatest success during your time with that company?
- What was your biggest failure on the job and what did you learn from it?
- Why do you think that this job is a better fit for you and your needs or goals?
- Why do you think you will be a good fit for this role?
- Why do you want to work for us?
- Please give me an example of how you have influenced others.
- Do you have any questions about this role?
- What do you expect to be doing in five years?
- Do you have any other interviews going on at the moment? Why do you want to join our organization?
- What would you do if xyz happened?
- Describe a situation in which you dealt with confrontation, for example, a difficult customer or a difficult colleague.
- What other careers have you considered or applied for?
- Why did you choose your degree subject?
- Describe yourself in one word.
- Are you prepared to be mobile? Are you willing to travel?
- Are you willing to work outside regular working hours?
- Describe a situation in which you showed initiative.
- Describe a situation in which you solved a problem.
- Describe a situation in which you took responsibility.
- What are your hobbies?
- What was your biggest setback? or How do you deal with adversity?

APPENDIX 2

Professionals interviewed for this book

Amina Malik (London, United Kingdom)

Amina is currently HR Director for an undisclosed London-based employer. Previous experiences include HR Business Partner at Genpact Headstrong Capital Markets, HR Officer at several financial organizations, including Origen, UniCredit Markets & Investment Banking, HSBC Investment Bank, and F&C Investments. Amina also volunteers for various projects and events that take place for the mayor of London.

Angelo Chirulli (London, United Kingdom)

With over ten years of recruiting, HR, tax, and management experience in multiple countries, Angelo currently works as Senior International Tax Associate and HR Advisor for LEXeFISCAL in Mayfair, London. He has also held multiple HR and management roles for several companies, including Eurobase, Pentasia, JBI Corporate Wealth Boutique, Motion International, Coin, Manpower, Erg, and Tim.

Antonio Iandolo (Düsseldorf, Germany)

General Manager Central Europe and Marketing Specialist for DB Apparel, Antonio has several years of experience managing large international teams. He has also worked at DIM, Playtex Europe, Sara Lee Branded Apparel, and Fater (Procter and Gamble Italy).

Cindy Anastasi (Malta)

An HR Specialist with over twelve years of experience in the field, she is currently HR Director at CCBill EU. Cindy has also worked as HR and Training Executive at InterContinental Hotels Group.

Cristiano Cardarelli, MBA (London, United Kingdom)

Cristiano is a business finance specialist in continuous improvement. With more than ten years of experience at multinational corporations, he has recruited, trained, and managed business specialists in large, complex environments. Currently employed as Excellence Manager (Downstream) in the energy sector, in the past he was Director of Finance and Operations at ESCP-Europe Business School in London. During his career, Cristiano has worked on challenging reorganization and outsourcing initiatives ranging from global strategic procurement to sales and supply deployment and service offshoring.

Daniel Singham (London, United Kingdom)

With more than ten years of experience in IT, management, and research, Daniel currently works as Client Services Team Leader at Toluna, one of the world's leading online panel and survey technology providers. He has also held positions at Pureprofile, Survey Sampling International, The London Borough of Hackney, and BT Global Services.

Delphine Lecluze (London, United Kingdom)

Currently HR Manager at Orient Capital, Delphine has more than ten years of HR management experience and has held positions at DF King, NYSE Euronext, Lombard Risk, and Garner International.

Faiz Nazerali (London, United Kingdom)

Managing Director of a London-based IT consultancy, Intellitech I.T. Solutions Ltd., Faiz has also worked as Senior Partner for Benco Holdings and IT Manager for Auto Parts & Service.

Julia Barber (London, United Kingdom)

Currently Managing Director Asia Pacific & London for Cornell Partnership, a recruiting company she founded more than ten years ago, Julia has also held positions at New Careers Revolution, The Eleven Minutes, EliteGraduateJobs, OxbridgeLife, and IQPC.

Julia Faida (Moscow, Russia)

A graduate of Westminster University in London, Julia has worked four years at Optimum Media OMD Group managing a team of three people.

Kelly Blokdijk (Orange County, California, United States)

Leveraging her unique perspective as a progressive thinker with a well-rounded background in diverse corporate settings, Kelly Blokdijk advises members of the business community on targeted HR, recruiting, and organizational development initiatives to enhance talent management, talent acquisition, corporate communications, and employee engagement programs. Kelly is an active HR and recruiting blogger and regular contributor to a variety of online industry communities. Follow Kelly on Twitter (@TalentTalks) or connect with her on LinkedIn.

Lisa Maghraoui (Washington, DC, United States)

Currently Director of HR for the Telecommunication Industry Association, Lisa has worked in HR for more than twenty years, including roles as HR Business Partner at Sprint and Director of HR at the National Automobile Dealers Association.

Luca Benigni (Rome, Italy; London, United Kingdom)

Luca has twenty-three years of management and legal experience at Benigni&K, an international law firm he founded and which currently has offices in London, Rome, Milan, and Bari.

Marco Sartarelli (Rome, Italy)

Business consultant for several healthcare and consumer goods companies, banks, and private equity firms, Marco is the owner of MS Partners and has also worked at Pulitzer Group, Colaplast, Astra

Farmaceutici, Centocor, and Menarini, managing teams of various sizes.

Michael O'Brien (New York, United States)

Currently Vice President Corporate Governance at BNY Mellon Depositary Receipts, Michael previously worked as Managing Director at Ipreo and Vice President at Citigate Dewe Rogerson.

Michael Witte (New York and Washington, DC, United States)

Currently Associate Director of Finance at Capgemini, Michael has also worked as Risk and Regulatory Reporting Manager at Hewlett-Packard and has served in various roles at Schering-Plough Corporation, PricewaterhouseCoopers, and Zarf Trust Corporation.

Mishelle Sassun (Tel Aviv, Israel)

Currently working in business development at Bee International, Mishelle has also worked in various management and marketing roles at companies including Definiti Media, DGM Mobile and Online Marketing, and Procter and Gamble.

Paolo Garonna (Rome, Italy)

Currently President of the Federazione Banche Italiane, Paolo Garonna is also a lecturer at LUISS Guido Carli University. He has served in roles such as Deputy Executive Secretary of the United Nations Economic Commission for Europe (UNECE), Director of the UNECE Statistical Division, General Director of the National

Statistical Institute of Italy (ISTAT) responsible for Italy's public statistics, Deputy Director for Manpower, Social Affairs, and Education at the Organization for Economic Cooperation and Development (OECD), and economic advisor to Ministers and Prime Ministers of Italy and other countries.

Stefano Bottaro (Rome, Italy)

An HR professional with fifteen years of experience in various HR functions in multiple industries, Stefano is currently HR Director at the Opera Theatre of Rome. He has also worked as HR Director at Alliance Medical, Bridgestone, Poste Italiane, and Radio Televisione Italiane (Rai).

Pritul Khagram (Wollaston, United Kingdom)

Founder and CEO of People Force International, Pritual is a Fellow of the Chartered Institute of Personnel Development (FCIPD) headquartered in London. An HR professional, he was previously HR Director at SOFGEN for nine years.

Sheryl Cuisia (London, United Kingdom)

Currently Managing Director and Founder of Boudicca Proxy, Sheryl has also worked as Senior Manager M&A Projects at Orient Capital, Head of Service Delivery and Senior Manager at Salisbury Associates, Account Manager Corporate Advisory at Georgeson, and Data Analyst Structured Finance at Standard & Poor's.

Tosin Ojikutu (Skipton, United Kingdom)

Currently Primary Servicing Oversight Manager at Investec, Tosin has also held various positions at Barclays, including Buy-to-Let Originations Team Leader, Consumer Affairs PPI Team Leader, Operational Manager Team Leader, and Knowledge Management Team Leader.

Victoria Barry-Woods (London, United Kingdom)

Victoria is an Account Director and award-winning recruiter working at Allegis Group, one of the largest privately held staffing companies in the world. She has eight years of experience with some of the most recognizable brands in consulting and industry. She also serves on the committee for the UK Healthcare Business Women's Association.

Dr. Vishwajeet Rana (London, United Kingdom)

Currently Chairman of Greensea Capital and Advisor for Global Banking Training School, Vishwajeet has also worked at various financial organizations, including HSBC and UBS Investment Bank.

www.ingramcontent.com/pod-product-compliance
Lightning Source LLC
Chambersburg PA
CBHW070812180526
45168CB00002B/590